Sexuality, learning difficulties and doing what's right

**Gavin Fairbairn, Denis Rowley
and Maggie Bowen**

David Fulton Publishers
London

David Fulton Publishers Ltd
2 Barbon Close, London WC1N 3JX
First published in Great Britain by
David Fulton Publishers 1995

British Library Cataloguing in Publication Data

A catalogue record for this book is available from the British Library

ISBN 1-85346-292-6

Typeset by The Harrington Consultancy Ltd
Printed in Great Britain by the Cromwell Press, Melksham.

Contents

Preface

This book has resulted from our awareness of the difficulties that professionals and parents face in accepting the sexuality of the people with learning disabilities with whom they live and work. It has been written at a time when discussion of such difficulties, and awareness of the prevalence of the sexual abuse of people with learning disabilities, is becoming more and more common. We believe the issues with which we deal are of enormous importance. Though they are difficult and distasteful at times, we hope you find what we have to say about them stimulating even though at times you may feel provoked and even shocked by some of what we have to say.

Acknowledgements

A number of friends and colleagues have helped us by sharing stories and experiences and listening to our developing ideas, and we are grateful to them. We are grateful also to our families for putting up with absentee parents for so much of the time over the past eighteen months. Susan Fairbairn deserves special thanks for her vigorous comments on a book in which at first she expressed no interest but in the end tells us she found enjoyable as well as thought provoking and at times upsetting. Though she often disagrees with what we have to say, she has helped us to say it more clearly. Finally, we are grateful to the staff of Pierre Lapin, Edinburgh who allowed two of us to work in the restaurant while we waited for it to open one evening towards the end of the writing of the book, after a traumatic day of computer problems which led us to travel from Dumfries to Edinburgh to seek help. Not only that, but they provided us with extra lighting to facilitate our work, and copious amounts of decent coffee to keep us awake, making us feel valued and looked after at a time when we needed positive strokes to keep going.

Language, labelling and political correctness[1]

In writing this book we have given a great deal of thought to questions about the language that we should adopt. For example, we thought long and hard about how we should refer to the people whose sexuality and lives we are discussing. In social work and health, terms like 'person with a mental handicap' or 'mentally handicapped person' have largely been replaced by the term 'person with a learning disability'. On the other hand, within education the term 'person with a learning difficulty' is perhaps more common. It is difficult to decide which of these two linguistic devices is better, more respectful, more accurate, more acceptable, more politically correct. It might be argued that to refer to a person as having a learning difficulty is preferable because to do so carries the implication that learning is possible; after all we all have difficulties in learning to some extent. By contrast, the argument would go, the term 'learning disability' has the disadvantage both that it implies a static state and also that its use gives discussion a medical flavour, as a result of which emphasis might be placed on pathology and deficiency rather than on the capacities and the possibilities for growth of the person in question.

Rather than adopting one at the expense of the other, we have decided to use the terms 'person with a learning difficulty' and 'person with a learning disability' interchangeably. We have done this partly because, although we favour the former term, we do not wish to offend against those who are committed to the latter; but partly we have done so because we believe that the attitudes that we develop and display towards any group or individual, and the ways in which we think about and relate to them, are even more important than the particular words we use.

Both terms present us with a problem of stylistic inelegance; for this reason we sometimes use the expression 'client' or 'clients' as a shorthand way of referring to people with learning difficulties/disabilities even when the people in question are still at school and it might be more usual to refer to 'children' or 'young people' or 'pupils'. Of course the term 'client' also has problems for those who are committed to political correctness or who wish to avoid criticism for speaking in ideologically inappropriate ways. It can be argued that to refer to people who use services as 'clients' is positive and empowering because of the association with areas such as the law where clients hire (and fire) those who provide services to them. However, the use of the term 'client' can also have negative connotations because of its associations with a paternalistic idea of the welfare system. Another term that we sometimes substitute for 'clients' is 'users', which in some ways is preferable because it is simply descriptive of the fact that the individuals in question are using services.

Related to the problem about how to refer to those people whose sexuality is being discussed in the book is the problem of how to refer to members of the mainstream population – those who do not have learning difficulties or disabilities. Here we find the term 'normal' offensive because it implies abnormality on the part of those who are excluded from that group, and normality is not a naturally occurring property of people but rather a social construct. In trying to find ways of avoiding the use of 'normal' we have used a variety of other expressions including 'regular', 'typical', 'ordinary', and 'average' (which we use in the sense implied in the phrase, 'the average person in the street', rather than intending any reference to, for example, IQ).

So we are anxious to mind the language that we use in order not to offend and, perhaps even more importantly from our point of view, in order to be clear in what we have to say. Sometimes, for the sake of clarity, we have chosen to use language that is archaic. For example, at times we refer to people as living in institutions or units for 'the mentally handicapped' or to 'mentally handicapped people' because this accurately reflects the terms that were used at the time and in the places that the stories originated, and not because we are insensitive or unaware that these are no longer the preferred terms. And seeking to avoid cumbersome forms of words we sometimes refer to the 'parents' of people with learning difficulties, when it would be more accurate to refer to 'parents or other home carers including, for example, other family members, friends or neighbours.'

Finally we have had to decide what to do about the problems that can be caused by gender specific language. Attention to gender awareness in language has become more and more important in academic writing in the social sciences and in practical areas such as social work and social policy. Indeed some publishers demand that authors adopt a variety of devices to avoid the exclusive use of male pronouns. We believe that it is important to avoid the offence that can be caused by the exclusive use of male forms and have given some thought to the best way to do so in this book. Rather than adopting common conventions which involve the exclusive use of plural pronouns or the use of the clumsy forms 'he/she' and 'his/hers', we have chosen, in so far as it has been possible to do so, to signal our awareness of the fact that there are both 'hes' and 'shes' in the world, by using masculine and feminine forms randomly.

Notes

[1] Most of our observations about language focus specifically on the conventions current in the UK. Had we written them with an eye on the language that is predominantly used in the USA or Australia, for example, we would have had to make different observations. However, the general point about attempting to find ways of speaking that are both accurate and inoffensive is universally valid and the problem of gender specific language is certainly relevant in other English speaking countries.

Sexuality as an ethical issue: a storytelling approach

In *Sexuality, learning difficulties and doing what's right* we draw both on our own experience and on the shared experience of others in addressing practical issues that arise in relation to the sexuality of people with learning difficulties. However, our main focus is an ethical one because many people find that sexuality causes them serious moral problems in living and working with people with learning difficulties. One of our major contentions is that in order to be able to act appropriately, it is essential that, as well as considering the practical issues of what to do, professionals and parents should give serious consideration to the ethical dimension; to the question, that is, of what *ought* to be done. For example, they must consider ethical questions such as these:

- What should be done about the fact that people with learning difficulties, as biological human beings, have sexual needs and feelings? Should they be encouraged in, or discouraged from, expressing these feelings and attempting to meet these needs?

- How should people with learning difficulties be helped to understand and grow in their sexuality? For example, whose values and aspirations should be paramount in determining how best to help any particular person with learning difficulties whether through informal support and friendship, or more formally through sex education and counselling? Should other people facilitate such a person's desires and needs in the area of personal and sexual relationships even when these do not accord with their own beliefs and values?

- How is it appropriate to act in relation to sexual behaviours of people with learning difficulties that are offensive to others? For example, what should be done about public masturbation and unwanted sexual advances of both a mild and a more serious kind?

- What can be done, and what ought to be done, in relation to the sexual abuse of people with learning disabilities? Particular problems here relate both to the extent to which abuse goes on between users of services, and to the possibility that professionals who, in permitting such abuse to go unnoticed, might be thought of not only as neglecting their duties but also, and more strongly, as actually abusing their clients. They also – and some people might consider this to be more serious – relate to occasions when clients are abused by those who are employed to care for them.

- How should we respond when problems arise in relationships and/or marriages between couples one or both of whom have learning disabilities? For example, is it reasonable to assume that any difficulties that arise do so solely because the partners have learning disabilities?

- How should society view situations in which people with learning difficulties enter into intimate sexual relationships with ordinary people? Are such relationships necessarily abusive? Is it right that, except where it occurs within marriage, sexual intercourse should be legally prohibited in such situations where the person with learning difficulties is a woman?

- How should society and its individual members view the possibility of long term sexual relationships between people with learning difficulties? In particular, how should we respond to the possibility that such relationships might lead to pregnancy and to not only parenthood but parenting, with or without marriage.

- Can it be right to sterilise people with learning difficulties or to arrange for them to be subjected to long term contraceptive control without their consent, and, if so, under what conditions? Related to this is the question of whether it can be any more right to use medication to control the sexual urges of people with learning difficulties than to do so to control those of any other person.

- How should we handle the problems that may arise if and when a woman with learning disabilities becomes pregnant? For example, is it acceptable that someone else should decide, on her behalf, that an abortion is required? Does anyone have the right to make this decision on behalf of another?

- A related question might arise when the father of an unborn child is a person with a learning difficulty. Should he have any say in the matter of whether or not his child should be brought to term and what should happen to it after it is born? Should it make any difference if the mother also has learning difficulties, and if the parents are not in a long term, committed relationship in which they jointly welcome the prospect of children? It is interesting, in passing, to consider whether fathers with learning difficulties should have any more right to determine their unborn child's future (even whether he/she has a future) than ordinary men who at the moment have little right to a say in this matter.

• If a couple, one or both of whom have learning difficulties, have founded a family and are having parenting problems, is it right that others, including social workers, should remove their child? Or at any rate, is it right that removal should be motivated partly because one or both parents have learning difficulties?

In this book we address these and other moral issues that sexuality raises; some we address in detail while others we do not focus on so closely but merely refer to tangentially. The fact that we do not give as much space to some issues – for example, to the problems that arise when a woman with learning difficulties becomes pregnant and abortion seems an 'obvious' solution – as we do to others, does not mean that we consider them to be less important. We hope that you will be encouraged to think about the issues that concern you most as you read what we have to say.

In raising the difficult issues that we explore, we use a storytelling approach both to illustrate points and to challenge you into thinking more closely about an area that is at times put to one side. The stories we use are of three different types: *real stories*, *imagined stories* and *hypothetical stories*.

Real stories recount actual events that happened to actual people. They are the kind of narratives that are often referred to as 'case studies' by social workers and doctors and psychologists and nurses. We find this label rather clinical; its use makes us think of scientific laboratories in which specimens are dissected and discarded. This is the reason that we prefer to work within the more humane tradition of storytelling both when we are talking about real lives and, as we shall describe presently, when we are talking about imagined and even hypothetical lives. Clinicians or practitioners who refer, for example, to diagnostic categories or dependency levels rather than to people with ailments or human problems in living, are able to remain somewhat remote from those whose lives constitute the cases to which they refer in their case studies. By contrast, storytellers live alongside and sometimes, vicariously at any rate, *inside* the stories they relate. Sometimes we make it obvious that a story really happened to a person we know or have known, or about whom we have heard from others; however, we have taken care to avoid identifying individuals whose lives still continue in the world outside this book.

Imagined stories are true to life tales about imagined lives and imagined people. Sometimes they are created by joining together threads from the lives of several people, bringing together actual events from actual lives. At other times they are entirely invented stories in which we use elements of our experience to bring particular issues into focus or in order to make some particular point clear; however, they always draw on our experience as individuals and as practitioners. In other words, although they are not real stories, they are *true*, at least in the sense that there are people – professionals and parents and carers, and people with learning difficulties – whose experiences and values and fears they reflect. And though the services to which they refer are not real, services with the values, beliefs and practices to which we refer in our imagined stories really do exist.

Finally, we tell *hypothetical* and sometimes far fetched stories of the kind that philosophers often use in their work. The use of hypothetical stories which highlight particular aspects of moral decisions and which are successively altered to focus attention is arguably the principal tool of the applied moral philosopher, and it is one that we will use from time to time. By using hypothetical stories in this way we hope we will not give the impression that we wish to make light of our topic. That we take it seriously will we hope be obvious from the fact that we do not shy away from making clear our strongly held views about some of the topics with which we deal and about the moral character of some of the real and imagined people who feature in our stories. Interestingly, although some of our stories are not only fictitious but far fetched and even outrageous, we have found that elements of them ring true with people who have read parts of the book as we have been working on it.

Sometimes the stories we use focus on individuals with learning difficulties; at other times they focus on their relatives or on professionals charged with their care. So for example, during the book we wil. be introducing you to the following people, some of whom we will visit only once, but some of whom we will visit on more than one occasion because their lives can help us to think about several of the more problems that sexuality raises:

> Tom, who was sterilised at the age of twelve when he was living in an institution for mentally handicapped people, and who at the age of twenty two, approached his family doctor with a view to having the procedure reversed.

Jane, who is about to begin attending a local FE College, and whose parents even at this stage won't allow their daughter to take part in sex education classes.

Alex and Jennifer, both of whom have Down's syndrome, who fall in love, court, move into a flat together, marry and then separate.

Phillipa, whose close attachment to her stepfather changed after her sixteenth birthday when he began to impose sex on her.

The staff at the social education centre that Graham attends, who are well meaning and open-minded about his developing relationship with his girlfriend Kate, but who act in ways that are less helpful and sensitive than they might be in relation to his needs and wishes.

Peter Green, who abused his position as a day centre officer to satisfy some of his perverse sexual interests by actions in relation to his clients that amounted to abuse of a non-contact kind.

The anonymous officers of the PPCA (The Parenthood, Parenting and Childcare Agency)[1] who pursue their duties to the best of their ability without questioning their moral rightness, even when they result in misery for the people in relation to whom they carry them out.

Beth, whose mother arranges for her to have a hysterectomy in order to save her the 'messy bother' of menstruation.

David, who was physically disabled and whose abuse at the hands of a group of older men in his mental handicap hospital was ignored by the staff over a period of years.

Jonathan, whose teachers found his habit of rubbing himself on furniture offensive and believed that his violent behaviour was the result of sexual frustration.

By working with stories that address issues in the lives of real and imagined people, we can develop ethical and personal sensitivity in thinking about the problems that sexuality can cause, in a way that allows us to relate helpfully to those who have experienced such problems in their lives. No matter how experienced we are in working with people with learning difficulties and how experienced at tackling problems relating to sexuality, we are all limited by our background and experience. Our moral imagination is formed in the lives we lead. Our values and ways of understanding depend on the ways we have been brought up and the experiences we have had. It is because our moral understanding is limited that, if we want to be ethical in our behaviour, we need to rehearse

10

decisions and reasons and justifications. Interacting with hypothetical and far fetched stories can enable us to clarify and sharpen up our ethical thinking. And interacting with stories that are either real or true to life though imagined, before we encounter them in the world, can be a good way of 'limbering' up for the real thing. We invite you to engage in some circuit training in the moral gymnasium we have tried to create – visiting and revisiting problems until you feel happy, or at any rate happier, with the prospect of encountering them or other similar problems, in your day to day life and work.

Notes

[1] We discuss the work of the PPCA in Part Four, where we address some of the ethical problems that can arise when people with learning difficulties become parents.

PART ONE

Ethics, learning difficulties and sexuality[1]

Sex and sexuality create problems. Sex worries us. It worries us because of the contradictory messages we receive about it. For example, most of us are bombarded on a daily basis with images on television and in the movies of the intense excitement and life enhancing quality of casual sexual encounters while at the same time, in the light of HIV and AIDS, we are reminded nearly as often of the dangers of such encounters both to ongoing relationships and family life, and to our health. In spite of its high profile in the media and the public consciousness, sex worries us because we find it embarrassing to talk about, and it worries us because we feel embarrassed about feeling embarrassed about talking about it. It is arguably because it worries us that problem pages in newspapers and magazines so often contain letters dealing with sexual matters. And it is not just the practice of sex in all its technicolour variety that is difficult, it is thinking and talking about it in a way that is mature and divorced from rudeness, innuendo or bravado, and from the over romantic ideals fostered by media portrayals of loving relationships.

The unease and embarrassment that we find in thinking and talking about sex arguably forms an unhelpful backdrop to the problems that the physical facts of sexuality can cause for those who are charged with the care of others. For example, in spite of the fact that sex is openly discussed on TV and radio chat shows at all times of day, and advertisements are carried in the media about safer sex and condoms, many parents are still reticent about discussing those *facts of life*, with their children.

In the minds of most people sexuality amounts to sex and in particular to sexual intercourse. This, when taken with the difficulties that we experience in discussing sex openly, may underpin the tendency to deny that some people, including disabled people, elderly people and what is more important in the context of this book, people with learning disabilities, are sexual beings. We do not intend to offer a lengthy discussion of the distinctions that are at times made between sex and sexuality, with sex usually being used in rather a limited sense to refer to physical acts and experiences and feelings, while sexuality is used to refer to a much wider area of human being and experiencing. We explore territory covered by both terms. Whether we choose to distinguish between them or not, these aspects of human life have such important implications for the lives of people with learning difficulties that many problems are caused simply by failing to address them adequately.

Denial of the sexuality of people with learning disabilities finds expression in many ways. For example, a parent might withdraw her teenager from sex education classes because she fears that this would lead to promiscuous behaviour. Or she might seek to prevent him masturbating, not only in public, but even in the privacy of his own bedroom, as if, by removing from her experience the evidence that he has sexual feelings and urges, she can change the fact that he is a sexual being. However, it is not only in relation to physical expressions of sexuality, or discussions of them, that denial occurs. Some parents may be so afraid of the possible physical consequences of allowing their child to develop sexually that they will seek to discourage, or even prevent, behaviour that though rooted in sexuality is not in itself overtly sexual. We are thinking here of young people with learning disabilities who are denied the opportunity to relate closely to another person with whom they identify in a boyfriend/girlfriend type relationship, despite the lack of risk that this in itself brings and the positive personal benefits that may follow from developing such a relationship.

To deny a person's sexuality is to deny part of her personhood; to deny that a person with learning disabilities is a sexual being is thus to treat her as less fully a person; and this is clearly an ethical issue. Of course, avoiding the sexual nature and sexual needs of people with learning difficulties is a matter of considerable practical importance. For one thing, such a person who is not informed about his or her sexuality, and of societal expectations relating to this aspect of human life, might behave in overtly sexual ways in public places and perhaps act over affectionately and inappropriately towards strangers, who may be shocked, offended, angered and even frightened by such attention. More importantly, if people with learning difficulties are not informed about relevant aspects of sex and sexuality, they may be more open to abuse from those who may seek to take advantage not only of their learning difficulties, and perhaps the naively trusting manner that others have unwisely or unwittingly cultivated in them, but also of their innocence in relation to sexual conduct. It is thus important that parents and others should be aware of and realistic about the fact that people with learning difficulties are sexual beings. Not only that but they must realise that people with learning difficulties may be perceived as potential sexual partners towards whom others may express interest and act sexually, whether or not they recognise the fact that they have learning difficulties. And naturally, therefore, educational and social work services need to be equipped and ready to support parents, teachers and care staff in developing such awareness.

Many of the most pressing problems about how to deal with sex, both as an educational issue and as an issue about practical caring, concern what one *can do and how one may do it*. However, we have found that many of the issues that colleagues raise in relation to the sexuality of people with learning difficulties are ethical issues – questions of right and wrong – about how it is appropriate to act, about what one *may do* and at times what one *ought to do*. We have been struck by the fact that when we ask colleagues what their most pressing problems are not only do they often pinpoint issues relating to sexuality but, when we push them further into explaining the nature of these problems, they often describe them in ways that suggest that the dilemmas they experience are moral in character. We are struck also by the fact that when, in approaching this area from another direction, we ask colleagues in the field to tell us about the ethical problems that cause them most pain, the issues they raise most often relate to sexuality.

As a result of their ethical worries the stories people tell often suggest that they feel frozen by their inability to handle the moral aspects of decision making, and hence action, in this area. This is true both of professionals and of those whose involvement is personal and relates, say, to a child or other relative. It is difficult enough for many people to take responsibility for the consequences of their own sexual decisions and choices let alone to do so for others, perhaps especially when they feel protective towards and responsible for them. Although this is true of everyone, things are perhaps particularly difficult for the practitioner who, in addition to his own sense of what is right, has the constraints of the law, societal expectations and agency policy weighing him down. Practitioners in work with people with learning disabilities often find sexuality difficult because although it is easy enough for them to obtain advice about *what can be done and how to do it,* it is less easy for them to obtain advice about the ethical problems that they experience. And so, for example, whereas they can go to a text or an authority to obtain help in deciding how best they might go about running sex education programmes, or how best they might attempt to modify inappropriate sexual behaviour, it is more difficult for them to get help in working out *what is morally acceptable* in doing so.

There are no guidebooks to right conduct in relation to the sexuality of people with learning difficulties; these are complex issues that reach right into the heart of the belief systems that parents and professionals hold dear and we do not propose to offer easy answers in this book. But though there are no guidebooks which give specific advice about what would and what would not be ethically acceptable behaviour in this area, many policy documents within organisations will contain, either explicitly or implicitly, moral comments or will to some extent have been underpinned by considerations of right and wrong.

It might be argued that there are no guidebooks to right conduct in the matter of sexuality for anyone, whether or not they have learning difficulties. There are, of course, guidebooks and videos about what one might do sexually, designed to spice up one's sex life, to which we all have easy access in the High Street; and it could be argued that implicitly at any rate these are also guides to right conduct because, in portraying and giving advice, even instruction in the matter of sexual behaviour, such guides rest on the assumption that the activities suggested and portrayed are proper. Indeed, like many agony uncles and aunts and many of those who from time to time offer advice about such matters on radio and television, the authors of such material are often at pains to point out that there is nothing that one might do sexually that is wrong, provided that no-one is hurt as a result. But acceptable conduct in sexual relationships is certainly as difficult to prescribe in relation to those who do not have learning difficulties as it is in relation to those who have, as one can see by looking at the problems that sex causes in all areas of private and public life.

So, although there are guidebooks to making one's sex life more exciting, there are no guides to ethics or even etiquette in the matter of sexual conduct. Even if there were, a guidebook to *doing what's right* in relation to the sexuality of others for whom one has responsibility would be different from one which addressed the ways in which decent individuals would think and act in respect of their own sexual needs and desires. It would be different because of the implications that might follow from becoming involved in the development and facilitation of sexual behaviour and feelings in others. Practitioners who have to deal with issues relating to the sexuality of others who have special needs as the result of physical disability and/or learning disabilities, face special problems because of the possibility that their conduct, however well meaning and however soundly based on research and solid experience, might be construed as improper. In this area their morality is as likely to come under close scrutiny as any professional expertise they may demonstrate in their work.

Sexuality as an ethical issue: redressing the balance

In the past, people with learning difficulties have not had the same range of opportunities in life that constitute the basis on which, without the use of guidebooks, regular people learn about friendship and relationships and which typically constitute a major plank in their learning about sexuality and sexual relationships. Perhaps largely as the result of the influence of *The Principle of Normalisation* (Wolfensberger, 1972) later redefined in terms of *Social Role Valorisation* (Wolfensberger, 1983), the idea that people with learning difficulties should be enabled to access the same opportunities as their ordinary peers is becoming more widely accepted. Though these ideas have created radical improvements for some individuals, the extent to which many people with learning disabilties are truly able to take control of their lives, and are encouraged and facilitated in doing so, remains questionable.

One result of the influence of the ideology of normalisation is that the friendship needs of people with learning disabilities are now beginning to be more generally recognised. For example, in their work on *circles of support*, Perske and Perske (1988) address relationship needs and in particular give detailed descriptions of some successful and enduring friendships between both adults and children with learning disabilities and their typical peers. They go so far as to suggest that such friendships can have a more powerful liberating effect on the lives of people with learning disabilities than anything that services have to offer. Indeed, when they wrote their book the Perskes took the view that friendships with regular citizens were the key to full integration for people with intellectual impairments. We are inclined to agree with them, although we believe that a fundamental change in the values of our society will be necessary before we can hope to reach a situation in which more intellectually able people and people with learning disabilities will routinely and regularly mix as friends in wholly mutual relationships.

Despite much investment in schemes designed to integrate people with learning difficulties in the community, and after the much publicised but barely effective move to integrate children with special educational needs with their regular peers in mainstream schools, the vast majority of people with learning difficulties still have relationship vacancies and their limited circle of friends tends to be made up of other people with learning difficulties. Not many people with learning difficulties have ongoing relationships with their typical peers and those who do rarely have relationships that can accurately be described as *real* friendships – by which we mean mutually affirming relationships. Even in areas in which a considerable investment of public money has been allocated to the development of schemes designed to integrate people with learning difficulties in all areas of life, success seems to have been difficult to achieve. For example, recent research in Wales (Davies and Jenkins, 1993) has suggested that over a decade after the All Wales Strategy for People with a Mental Handicap began, the friendship patterns of people with learning difficulties in Wales have not changed. [2]

There is now a considerable body of literature relating to sexuality and people with learning disabilities both in the UK and elsewhere (see, for example, Craft, 1993; Monat-Haller, 1992, and a special issue of *Mental Handicap*, 1992). There is a surfeit of teaching and training packages about aspects of sexuality aimed both at addressing the training needs of professionals and carers and for use in work with young people with learning disabilities; some of these, as well as offering their own version of guidance about what one might do, provide a list of resources and organisations working and publishing in this area (see, for example, McCarthy and Thompson, 1992). However, even though sexuality in relation to people with learning disabilities is an area of growing interest in academic and informed professional circles, the fact that their clients are sexual beings still causes many of the most important practical and ethical problems for staff in services. It is clear from the briefest of overviews of the literature, that much work has been and is being done, about practical approaches in this area. However, although references are occasionally made to what *should* be done, the dominant focus of this literature tends to be on empirical findings and pragmatic issues, that is, about what *can and is being done.*

We want to attempt to redress the balance by focusing specifically on the ethical dimension of issues relating to the sexuality of people with learning disabilities.

Ethics and morals

Some people might think that a consideration of ethics in this area is a bit of a luxury: interesting but inessential, and rather divorced from practice. They are likely to believe that a book addressing moral issues could not be practical in nature. Faced with the problems of practice, they might argue that they are so fully occupied with questions about what *can be done*, that they are unable to give up time to thinking about what *ought to be done*. Against those who see ethics as a non-essential frill, we would argue that a consideration of the ethical problems that sexuality raises in the field of learning difficulties is central to practice.

Other people might find themselves rejecting a consideration of ethics, particularly in relation to questions of sex, because they have confused a consideration of ethical issues with the crime of 'moralising', in which one person who claims to hold the moral high ground tries to bully others into behaving in ways that she considers morally acceptable. Such people may view any consideration of morality as being essentially about one lot of people – usually those in power – wanting to impose their standards on others in a 'back to basics', paternalistic and reproving kind of way. Examples of this moralising approach to morality are to be found in those newspaper headlines that one often sees, in which politicians, bishops and other dignified and societally approved exemplars of moral conduct are said, for example, to have made statements about how they 'deplore the falling moral standards among the young'. They are also to be found in the attacks that young people often make on what they take to be their 'ignorant' elders[3] who are less politically aware and less well versed, for example, in arguments concerning animal rights, environmental ethics and the rights of minority groups such as gay people, ethnic minorities and people with disabilities.

Ethics is sometimes confused with two other areas: etiquette and the law. By *etiquette* we mean doing the right thing in the sense of acting politely. Thus, for example, there are rules of etiquette or politeness that govern life in general and there are rules of etiquette that govern specific occasions. Included in etiquette are requirements about ways of addressing people of a particular status both in the flesh and in writing, requirements about which piece of cutlery one must use at each stage in a formal meal (and what one may do with it) and, in professional circles, about how one must be respectful to one's boss even if he/she is a buffoon. But though politeness is a virtue it is not necessarily morally right.

Nor is it necessarily morally right always to obey the law; the law can be an ass. Consider, for example, a law which required citizens to provide information about everyone they knew who was heterosexual (or homosexual) or who liked a particular pop group, because such individuals, by Act of Parliament, had been declared criminal and furthermore that their offences were punishable by death. Such a law would be not only foolish but immoral, just as certain aspects of the law pertaining to sexual orientation have been, and to our way of thinking still are, morally mistaken. Or at least a law of this kind would be immoral unless it could be shown that there was some morally defensible reason for punishing heterosexuals (or homosexuals) or supporters of the pop group in question. If, for example, it could be demonstrated that not only could sexual orientation be chosen but that choosing the one that had been criminalised had very bad effects on others, or that supporting the pop group in question somehow had similarly bad effects on other people, then punishment for these new 'offences' might be justifiable. On the other hand, the bad effects they caused would have to be severe and constitute more than mere aesthetic offence; and a separate argument would have to be given in favour of capital punishment rather than, for example, imprisonment. Of course, there is a close connection between ethics and the law because in general the law is closely related to commonly shared moral beliefs. But this is not necessarily so. And so although in general we believe that it is wise and proper for people to obey the laws of the country in which they live, it is at least arguably better that a person should disobey the law if by doing so she will be acting in ways that she considers to be morally correct, than that she should act in accordance with a law that she considers to be morally corrupt.

A distinction is sometimes made between 'ethics' and 'morals' or 'morality', with 'ethics' being used to refer to the systematic study of morality in terms of the principles that may be used in practical moral decisions, and 'morals' or 'morality' being used to refer to the situations, actions, beliefs, attitudes, and so on, to which ethical theories are a systematic response. Used in accordance with this distinction, *ethics* is thus more abstract than *morality*. However, the terms 'ethics' and 'morality' are often used interchangeably both by philosophers and non-philosophers and we are not committed to distinguishing between them. When we talk about the ethical or moral problems that arise in relation to the sexuality of people with learning difficulties, what we intend is to focus attention on the kinds of questions that you might find yourself discussing using words like 'right' and' wrong', 'good' and 'bad'; acts and actions that might be thought proper and improper; things that should be done and things that ought not to be done.

We are not concerned to argue for a particular school of ethical thought, in favour, for example, of a utilitarian or a Kantian approach to ethics; nor are we concerned to offer, as many books about ethics for practitioners do, a potted guide to various ethical theories – a kind of 'Bluff Your Way in Ethics'. This seems to us to be less relevant than the attempt to uncover and spell out in plain language the kinds of moral issues that are faced by those who encounter the reality of sexuality as an aspect of the lives of people with learning difficulties.[4] We want to encourage you to consider the moral questions that sexuality raises in relation to such people.

In thinking about the issues we raise in this book, we invite you to think carefully about the kinds of things that follow from particular beliefs that you hold, if you hold to them consistently. Sometimes, when we realise that beliefs we hold have implications that we had not considered, we modify our beliefs. Consider for example, the way in which Steven finds his views changing in the following story:

> Steven has always maintained the view that abortion is a woman's right to choose, that the child before birth is not yet a person and that a woman should thus be permitted to choose abortion on any grounds.
>
> One evening in his extra-mural philosophy class, Steven's tutor challenges him to justify his liberal views about abortion. During the discussion that ensues, she asks whether he thinks that a woman who wants to look stunning at a ball should be permitted to have an abortion in order to arrange that she can fit into her most elegant evening gown; she asks also whether he thinks that it is right that a couple should be permitted to abort their baby because antenatal screening has shown that it does not come up to the gender specification that they have laid down for it – say, that she is a girl when what they want is a boy. Steven replies that he doesn't believe that abortion on either of these grounds should be allowed; further than that, he says that he thinks that to abort babies for such trivial reasons is disgusting and immoral.
>
> When he goes to the pub with his friend after the evening class, she challenges Steven to justify the view that he expressed in class, given the absolutist positions she knows he has always put forward in the past about 'a woman's right to choose'. He reflects for a while and then restates his position on abortion in the following terms:
>
> 'Women should be permitted to choose abortion only when they have a very serious reason for doing so.'

Reflection on the question about the woman who wants to wear her elegant evening gown to the ball and on the possibility that abortion of babies might be sought and permitted simply because they are of the wrong sex has made Steven shift his ground by bringing in qualifications to cover his reaction to the idea that a woman might have an abortion for what he considers to be trivial reasons. It may be that reflecting on these stories has brought about a fundamental change in his underlying beliefs and that he now believes abortion to be wrong in most circumstances because, for example, it involves the death of a person and therefore should not be carried out unless the woman's life is gravely threatened by continuing with the pregnancy. On the other hand he may still consider the unborn baby not to be a person. In that case his reason for changing his view might be that though he still believes abortion is a woman's right he believes that its implications for marriage and relationships give it such importance that he now thinks it is something that should not be

undertaken for such a trivial reason. Whatever the truth of the matter, being faced with a far fetched and some would say outrageous hypothetical scenario and with a not so far fetched though some would think equally outrageous real-life scenario has made Steven reassess his beliefs in the light of the conflicting values he holds about the freedoms to which he thinks women should be entitled and the value of life and relationships.

The ethical territory ahead: a sketch map of the book

In our discussions of the stories we have chosen to present in this book, we cover a wide range of human experience and a wide range of attitudes towards sexuality. We touch on significant ethical qualms and taboos relating to sex (and thinking about sex) in relation to people with learning difficulties, and on public attitudes towards the idea that like their ordinary peers people with learning difficulties have sexual feelings and needs. In doing so we examine some of the myths that surround views about people with learning difficulties, not only in relation to their sexuality but in relation to their ability and inclination to form close relationships. In other words, our concerns are wider than simply a discussion of sexuality conceived in terms of physical relationships. Our exploration of sexual relationships is thus related to other aspects of human relationships such as friendship formation. We are concerned also with the risks to which people with learning difficulties are exposed whether in institutions, the home or in the community. Their vulnerability means that they may be open to sexual abuse in all of these contexts.

Some of the most upsetting and unsettling problems that arise in relation to the sexuality of people with learning disabilities arise at the transition from childhood to adulthood when, for example, parents and professionals must strike a balance between facilitating informed and responsible decision making and taking the risks that are involved in doing so. However, it is important to remain aware that the sexual nature of people means that those who are involved with individuals with learning disabilities are likely to be faced with dilemmas of a sexual nature whatever the age of the person in question. So, for example, the parents of a five year old might be concerned and worried about what they should do about her constant habit of lifting the skirt or fondling the breasts of any woman she meets; and the staff charged with responsibility for a small group of older adults in supported accommodation might find the fact that two of the residents wish to leave and set up home together as a couple, quite challenging.

The issues we address are of interest and concern to professionals in health, education and social services and to parents and family carers who have daily contact with people with learning difficulties, and it is our ambition that the book might contribute to, and perhaps even stimulate, ethical debate in such situations. They are undoubtedly of concern also to many people with learning difficulties and we hope that the book may prove of some use to advisors of self advocacy groups working with problems in this area.

Notes

[1] Some of the ideas that we develop in this book were first raised in a series of columns in the *SLD Experience* (British Institute of Learning Disabilities) in 1993 and 1994.

[2] The All Wales Strategy is a Welsh Office initiative (Welsh Office, 1983, 1993) based on the principles of normalisation which is aimed at providing people with learning difficulties with the same kind of opportunities as everyone else.

[3] 'Ignorant' in this context is intended to suggest that the people in question are uneducated about the issues rather than that they are ignorant in the more usual and derogatory sense of the word; however helpful it might be for bigots, to have simple rules of thumb in this area, neither age nor any other distinguishing feature, including political persuasion, is a sure guide to ignorance of this kind.

[4] Those who wish to pursue moral theory and its application to practical situations more closely may wish to have a look at Gillon (1986); Arras and Hunt (1983); Beauchamp and Childress (1994); Campbell (1972).

PART TWO

Sweet little mystery: the person with learning difficulties as a sexual being

We can't avoid sex and sexuality. It is there whether we like it or not. It is there in our lives and in our bodies. For most of us it is there in our experience – in our feelings and desires, in our hopes and in our fears, in our waking and quite probably in our sleeping. We might be able to draw a curtain over our sexuality, to hide it from view, to deny it; but we can't get rid of it. Nor can we get rid of the sexuality of the people with learning difficulties with whom we live and work. We may deny it or accept it; draw a curtain over it or work with it. But we cannot get rid of it. Rather we have to respond to it in some way and in Part Two we discuss the range of responses that are possible.

The impact of considerations about sexuality on the lives of people with learning difficulties and on the lives of those who live and work with them is obvious. However, this aspect of their lives has often been ignored. As a result the issues that arise in this area are handled in ways that are often based not on knowledge but on a mythology that has been passed from generation to generation; a mythology based on fear and misunderstanding and the need to control. Myths and misconceptions about people with learning difficulties are common currency. They are often described as 'perpetual infants' who live in a state of grace, a permanent and holy innocence; but at the same time they may be viewed as a taint on our society, a threat to the intelligence of the nation, a danger to the gene pool. Because of the idea that they exist in perpetual childhood it is common for them to be thought of as not men/not women and therefore not sexual, even when they are physically mature. And yet at the same time adults with learning difficulties may be thought of and characterised as being sexually menacing – as having urges that are beyond their capacity to control.

Myths and misconceptions of the kind we have alluded to result in an unfortunate and damaging trade in tales that stereotype people with learning difficulties and restrict the public view of them. Along with these, the way in which people react to the sexuality of a person or group of people with learning difficulties will be influenced by personal experience, by religious and moral beliefs, by conceptions of disability and in particular of people with learning difficulties; it will also depend on their view of the place and importance of sexuality within human life.

Thus there is a wide range of beliefs and values in relation to sexuality and learning difficulties. There is no straightforward division in the way that these beliefs and values, and the actions that are consequent on them, are distributed. For example, it is not simply the case that families, being intensely and emotionally involved, are restrictive, whereas staff working within human services, being more educated and knowledgeable, are more liberal. In the stories we will share in this book there are examples of situations in which helpful support is offered to people with learning difficulties in respect of their sexual development, not only by professionals, but by parents; and there are others in which the lack of support, or badly judged support, has negative results.

The conservative and liberal views of the sexuality of people with learning difficulties

The wide range of factors – experiences, beliefs, myths, values, understandings and misunderstandings – that form our views of sexuality and of the place of sexuality in the lives of people with learning disabilities, can lead to a confusing and often contradictory range of ways of responding to their emerging and developing sexuality in childhood, adolescence and adulthood. They can range from denial to acceptance; from embarrassment to celebration; from putting up with to brutal intrusion upon.

In approaching the problems and dilemmas with which they are faced, both parents and professionals are limited by their background, by their values and experiences, by their understanding and by their hopes and fears. As a result, their responses to the sexuality of the people in their care and the ways in which they respond to particular situations and crises reflect a continuum of opinion which may, in a general way at least, be characterised as having liberal and conservative poles.

The conservative view

Those who occupy the conservative pole of this continuum believe that it is inappropriate to allow or encourage people with learning difficulties to express any sexual feelings. The conservative point of view may manifest itself in a number of different ways. Consider, for example, the following brief vignettes from the lives of some real and imagined people:

> Karen is a twenty year old woman who lives in a residential community for people with learning difficulties run by a religious organisation. The house is equipped and furnished to the highest possible standard but is located in an isolated rural setting. The staff of the community are a mix of paid staff and young, mostly foreign, volunteers. The policy of the organisation places particular emphasis on the need for staff to be celibate in order that the role models they provide for residents will be pure. As if to emphasise this policy further, the community is resisting pressure from the statutory authorities to introduce single rooms for residents.

> Mavis Harrington's sixteen year old daughter, Jacinta, spends very little time with her peer group outside school because she has always enjoyed spending time with her mum – helping round the house, attending embroidery class, and going to Women's Institute meetings where she learns about baking and making jam and so on. Mrs Harrington always says that she is glad that Jacinta enjoys being with her so much, especially now that she is growing up and should be doing more and more grown up things. An added benefit from Mrs Harrington's point of view is that while they are together her daughter is not being exposed to other possibly harmful influences and situations, including boys and men. Of course, her husband Fred agrees with her views about keeping Jacinta out of harm's way.

> Mr and Mrs Stafford want what's best for their daughter Jane. They have always kept her well dressed and groomed; they have given her a full life. The problem for the Staffords is that Jane is about to leave school to attend a link course at a local college where she will come into contact with a different kind of youngster from those she has grown up with in her special school. It is not that they don't welcome the broadening of Jane's horizons, but they do worry a little about some of the things they have heard about the college's approach to growing up. They are also worried about some of the risks that Jane will face now that she is becoming a woman.

> Irene attends a large day school for pupils with moderate and severe learning difficulties where her individual programme includes work on 'life skills'. As well as instruction in budgeting, shopping, and cooking, this programme includes attendance for two sessions a week on a personal, social and moral education course as part of which a health education officer is teaching twelve sessions of sex education. Irene's parents are unaware that she is participating in this course and would be unhappy if they were to find out.

John's parents, recognising that their son is growing up, have started involving him in more of their own social activities. Acknowledging that he is growing into an adult and should have the opportunity to mix with other adults, his mother has begun taking him to coffee mornings and whist drives at church, while his dad occasionally takes him to the pub or to football matches. They do not, however, encourage John to spend time with his friends from school or even to join in any of the activities in the neighbourhood in which other teenagers tend to engage – youth clubs and so on. Indeed, on the few occasions that John has been invited to spend time with friends of his own age, his parents have always managed to make available alternative activities that he is likely to enjoy more. Perhaps as a result, the few friendships he had with local people of his own age have slowly withered away. Although they have never talked about this properly, both parents are glad that John enjoys being with them so much because they have always worried about how they would manage when he got to this age and began wanting to have a girlfriend.

Shirley, a mild and unusually co-operative person, lives in a residential care home for elderly people, in a small town. She was placed there eleven years ago when she was anything but old, because the lack of appropriate facilities meant that the social services department could not think what else to do with her. She is now forty eight and over the past three years she has become increasingly involved in the local self advocacy group. It was through this group that she first met Patrick, a younger man with learning difficulties. Though they have been going together for eighteen months the staff at the care home are unhappy about Shirley bringing Patrick home with her and will not allow them to spend time alone in Shirley's room. At first Shirley reacted to this paternalistic control of her life by becoming depressed about it. Recently, however, she has begun to show signs of anger and there have been several episodes in which she has aggressively demanded her right to a bit of privacy.

These stories illustrate a range of possible responses to the sexuality of people with learning difficulties that could be characterised as conservative, from the attempt actively to prevent sex becoming an issue through to the failure to discuss or even think about it. Some parents and care staff whose beliefs and values fall towards this end of the spectrum attempt to create a kind of asexual social order around the people for whom and towards whom they have responsibility. One example of this may be found in the residential community in which Karen lives, where, for ideological reasons relating to their beliefs about the nature and potential of people with learning difficulties, the staff believe that it is best to keep their residents innocent of sex so far as is possible. It is not that they wish to deprive their residents of a worthwhile aspect of human experience but rather that they believe that since the kind of person they care for is incapable of dealing with the complications that sex can bring it is better if their lives are not tainted with it.

The subtle manoeuvres in which the Harringtons have engaged in an effort to prevent Jacinta coming into contact with men and the possibility of sexual danger are another example of the attempt to de-sexualise the world in order to protect a person with learning difficulties. Not only are they involving Jacinta in their social lives to an extent that would be unacceptable to most adolescents, but they are doing so in an effort deliberately to keep her away from her peer group, away from boys and men, and out of harm's way. Funnily enough, unlike many parents who share similar fears, the Harringtons have never attempted to prevent Jacinta participating in sex education classes though they have tried to stop her thinking about boyfriends, and have always worried about the way television can put ideas into young people's heads. Part of their motivation for allowing her to take part in sex education at school was that when Jacinta was beginning her periods Mavis found it invaluable to have the help of the teachers in explaining what was going on. In a way, the fact that Jacinta has had so much sex education over the years has contributed to her parents feeling as worried as they are about what she might get up to if they let her out of their sight.

The Staffords, like the Harringtons, firmly believe that the best way to protect their daughter against many of the possible evils of adult life is to try as far as they can to limit her exposure to sex. And so they have tried to avoid her being exposed to portrayals of sex on TV and in the papers. Unlike the Harringtons, however, they have also tried to prevent Jane hearing about sex from her peers both locally and at school. They do not want to admit that their daughter is a sexual being, and are so anxious to prevent her being exposed to such matters that throughout her school life they have demanded that she be excluded from all sex education classes. They intend that this will also be the case when Jane starts college.

Like the Staffords and the Harringtons, Irene's parents want to avoid their daughter coming into contact with sex because they don't want her to get involved with that kind of thing. In order to protect her they have have tried to ensure that she has as little contact with men as possible except when they are doing things as a family or when she is in the care of her teachers who they trust to keep her safe. After all, getting too interested in men at an early age can have drastic consequences, especially for a girl like Irene who is too trusting and too willing to please. Again, like the Staffords and the Harringtons, they have worked hard at avoiding her coming into contact with portrayals of sex on TV and it is because they are so anxious to maintain their daughter's innocence of sex that they have always steadfastly refused to allow her teachers to include Irene in sex education classes.

Irene's parents are committed to doing what's best for their daughter.

They want to protect her. At the same time, the teachers and other staff at Irene's school are also anxious to do what's best for her. However, unlike her parents they do not believe that Irene's interests will be best served by depriving her of sex education. They are convinced that she should learn something about sex especially since she seems to be becoming interested in some of the older boys in the school. It is because they are concerned about her mild mannered willingness and her trusting nature that they have decided that whatever her parents think and want they must ensure that Irene has sufficient knowledge of sex to be able to make decisions about what she wants, if and when she finds herself in situations where sex becomes an issue. That is why they are prepared to risk the wrath of her family by neglecting to inform them about the course in which Irene is participating.

Irene's story is an example of the way in which things can go wrong between parents and professionals when they do not communicate openly about their disagreements. Although they do not have a conflict of interest, the staff and Irene's parents have different views about what they should do to protect Irene from possible harm. It is clear that the staff have acted with the best of intentions. And it is clear that Irene's parents have had the best of intentions in trying to avoid her being exposed to the kind of sex education programme she is now receiving without their knowledge. Are the staff right to be doing what they are? Doing so avoids the drama and perhaps trauma of confrontation with Irene's parents and perhaps a legal battle if their disagreement were to lead to a court case over who could best look after Irene's interests. We can understand why the staff should wish to avoid a dispute over what is best for Irene and we can understand that they want to do what they consider is best for her. However, in our view, though we agree strongly with their analysis of the situation, we think that they are mistaken and even morally wrong to have taken the action that they have.

To some extent John's parents could be viewed as making an active attempt to help their son in establishing an adult identity for himself. On the other hand, although they have probably not intended to do so, it could be argued that by failing to encourage him to develop interests outside the family they are failing to acknowledge his needs as an adolescent. No doubt by doing their best to involve him in adult activities they think they are encouraging him to grow up. But it could be argued that by failing to support his requests to be allowed to go and spend time with his peers on occasions when he has been invited to do so, they have denied him the opportunity to develop the ability to make informed choices between the coffee mornings and the pub; or between going with dad to the football, and going with his friends to the youth club. And it is certainly true that they are denying him the experience of average adolescent boys – youth clubs and mixing with girls and so on. On the surface there seems to be nothing about their behaviour to suggest that considerations about sex have played any part in their deliberations and decisions about how to act, though it might well be the case that at a subliminal level their reasons for keeping John close to home stem from barely imagined fears relating to his obvious sexual maturity – about what he might do, or what might happen to him, if they were not with him.

The attitudes displayed by John's parents are in some ways similar to those demonstrated by Mr and Mrs Harrington in relation to Jacinta, which we have already discussed, because both sets of parents are anxious to involve their youngster in adult activities and both at the same time are glad that in this way they can avoid the complications that the possibility of boyfriends/girlfriends might cause. The approaches to growing up taken by both Jacinta's parents and John's parents have resulted in lifestyles for these young people that have some similarity to the lifestyles that result from the approach taken by the staff of the residential community in which Karen lives. In each of these stories sexual risk is avoided by strategies of friendship prevention. But whereas John and Jacinta are isolated from their peers while living in the community, Karen is allowed and encouraged to mix with her immediate peers while being segregated from the wider community. In her case, what is important is not the absence of peer contact, and in particular contact with other young people of the opposite sex, but that she and her fellow residents are being given a model of human behaviour that is essentially celibate and non-sexual. For her it is not friendships *per se* that are discouraged, but friendships that could develop a sexual component.

In Shirley and Patrick's case, sexual risk is also avoided. There are some parallels between their circumstances and those of Karen, though in this instance the staff do not model a celibate lifestyle, but simply attempt to prevent intimacy taking place. The staff of the residential care home where Shirley lives have taken recourse to rules and regulations about segregating men and women in separate bedrooms in order to justify their actions. They have done this in spite of the fact that nowadays not only are men and women who live in supported accommodation services for people with learning difficulties more likely to be offered a single room, but that the ethos that underpins such services makes it more likely that they will have freedom about who they can have as visitors in their rooms.

Shirley has fallen foul of conservative and rule bound practice. She has been inappropriately placed in a residential care home for elderly people and, in addition to this, the home in which she has been placed has a particularly restrictive regime, as a result of which she and Patrick are being denied opportunities for privacy. Furthermore, they are being denied such opportunities because the management of the home disapprove of the idea of residents having sex together. That is why they have made no move to provide double rooms for married couples; and it is why they will not allow Patrick to enter Shirley's bedroom. It seems to us to be an insult for the staff to make decisions about what Shirley and Patrick might do together in private unless invited to do so or unless there is good reason to believe that what they are likely to do will be either harmful or illegal. If Shirley and people like her are to be allowed to live their lives in a dignified and life enhancing way, the staff who have responsibility for them need to show some flexibility in how they respond. Rules that do not allow Shirley to have a visitor of the opposite sex in her room are entirely inappropriate. The lack of a private place is a very real restriction on Shirley and Patrick and, even if there are rules placing limitations on who can spend time in whose bedroom, the staff will not be doing right by them if they continue to prevent this couple from having a private space and private time together.

It is perhaps paradoxical that the rules and regulations to which the staff are appealing in order to avoid the possibility of a sexual relationship developing between Shirley and Patrick could have the odd result that they facilitated a woman like Shirley in developing a lesbian relationship with one of the other women in the group home, or even with a friend from the outside world. It is paradoxical because it is likely that the staff would find such a relationship even more difficult to cope with than the relationship between Shirley and Patrick to which they are attempting to put paid.

The liberal view

The other end of the continuum of opinion about the ways in which it is appropriate to think about and act in relation to the sexuality of people with learning difficulties is occupied by those who believe that since people with learning difficulties have a right to a sex life those who are charged with caring for and assisting them in their growth towards living life as fully and as independently as possible should do what they can to assist in this area, just as they should in all other areas. As was the case at the other end of the continuum, there are different approaches to fulfilling this aspiration.

Let us begin by looking at some stories in which positive steps are taken to support people with learning difficulties as they develop their lives as sexually mature people.

Alex and Jennifer both have Down's syndrome. They have been good friends ever since they met at the local special school that they attended. Their friendship continued when they both moved on to the local adult training centre (ATC). Now in their thirties and with the support of both families, they are planning their wedding. Afterwards they are going to live as husband and wife with Alex's parents until they can find a place of their own. Neither Jennifer nor Alex has ever lived away from the family home and their plans to marry and set up home together were at first a great shock to both sets of parents, neither of whom would have predicted this outcome to the long term friendship that Alex and Jennifer have enjoyed.

William Park lived in a large mental handicap hospital for over twenty years having been admitted there as a child. Ten years ago, with the assistance of a local voluntary organisation, he successfully moved out into his own flat and has held down a job as a gardener ever since. It was through his work that he met Mary, a woman without learning difficulties who lived in a tied cottage on the large estate where he is employed and to whom he has been married for five years. Now that Mary is expecting their first child, the voluntary organisation has helped them to find a bigger house through a local housing association.

Loriel is ten years old and lives in a residential school. Recently one of the care staff, noticing that she is developing 'into a young woman', bought her a bra. Unfortunately, although she was delighted to receive this gift, Loriel has no idea what she is supposed to do with it.

Alex and Jennifer are unusually lucky as a couple in having the support of both of their families in planning their marriage and life together. Like many young couples they are going to live with one set of parents when they get married. From their point of view and that of their parents who are supporting them in their plans to marry and live together independently, this arrangement will bring benefits. The newly weds will have help in establishing their marriage by having some of the practical problems that face most young couples suspended for a while. For their part, both sets of parents will have the security of knowing that for a time at least their children will have a guiding hand to help them as they grow in confidence in the everyday routines of independent adult life together. Of course, as is the case with any couple who live with parents for a time, there are dangers as well as benefits to be gained from living under a parental roof. However, for Jennifer and Alex the benefits outweigh the hazards.

Like Alex and Jennifer, the Parks were fortunate enough to be surrounded by people who really wanted them to succeed as they married and settled down together. Unlike Alex and Jennifer however, neither William nor Mary had any close family members willing to give the support that they needed both to undertake the move towards establishing themselves as a couple and in overcoming the prejudice that they met in doing so. Rather, their support came from the voluntary agency that helped William move into the community and from the circle of friends he and Mary had developed. They are now well established as a couple, and from Mary's point of view their relationship has brought many benefits. Her marriage to William continues to be happy; she is pregnant, pregnant by choice with the man she loves, and very much looking forward to parenthood, and she has a greater feeling of security about her accommodation than she had during the years that she was tied to a home provided by her workplace. To her, William's wasted years in an institution seem incomprehensible.

In the case of the Parks and of Jennifer and Alex, the adoption of a liberal position led to good interventions that were experienced by each of the couples as helpful and positive. However, the liberal view can also lead to unhelpful interventions. Consider, for example, the unqualified care assistant who bought Loriel her first bra and surreptitiously gave it to her without explanation as to its function. No one seems to have been clear about just whose job it was to advise Loriel about the changes going on in her body and to assist her in coming to terms with them. As a result, this thoughtful but unthinking member of staff went beyond her remit in interfering in what was really a job for a teacher or qualified member of care staff. Though she did not have any direct responsibility for Loriel, she had observed her growing up fast but was embarrassed and confused by the fact that her professional colleagues had done nothing about it. Had the school been a place where professional and educational matters were more openly and clearly discussed, it would have been possible for her to bring her concerns to the attention of those who were more qualified to take action and they might then have had a more positive effect. As it was, she was acting out of care and concern by doing her best to help Loriel with the problems of growing up. However, in the absence of any instruction or even of less formal advice about the purpose of this strange garment, it is destined to cause upset and worry – perhaps embarrassment – for this pubescent youngster. And so, despite the fact that this care assistant took a relatively liberal view of sexual development, and in good faith did her best to help, the failure of the professional staff to deal openly with this issue and their failure to clarify roles and responsibilities has had the result, not only that Loriel continues to be uninformed regarding her sexual maturation, but that she is feeling confused and anxious about her new gift.

Liberal intentions can lead to even more questionable activities than the rather coy provision of a bra. Consider, for example, the following story in which the attempt to assist a young person in developing his sexual identity turns into behavioural imposition.

> Graham attends a social education centre for people with learning difficulties; he has a steady girlfriend and the staff of the centre are keen to be supportive to him. The work of the centre is based upon the principles of normalisation and the staff are proactive in helping users to fulfil socially valued roles. They routinely provide a carefully constructed programme of appropriate sex education to all members of the centre but believe that with someone like Graham, who is doing so well in establishing himself in the community and developing his relationship with his girlfriend Kate, they should go a bit further in helping him to come to terms with his sexual role as a man. As a result of these features of the ideology and commitments underpinning the practice of the centre, the staff are thus helping Graham to learn about 'what to do' sexually.

The staff of his social education centre are trying to assist Graham in developing his identity as a sexually mature man. They are committed not only to the idea that he has the right to a fulfilled sex life but to the fact that however challenging to them personally and professionally it is part of their job to assist in this area. However, although they are motivated to do what's best for Graham, they have failed to take sufficient advice about how to proceed. As a result, the approach they have adopted and the goals they have set for their work with Graham are rather limited in scope and involve using a manual of illustrations showing couples engaging in sexual intercourse, to give him guidance about 'what to do'. The fact that the approach they have adopted and the targets they have set for their work are inappropriate for him, is an illustration of their limited understanding both of Graham and of the nature of human sexuality.

The decision to embark upon this particular course of action without fully talking things through with Graham was perhaps taken because the staff felt unsure how to discuss such a delicate matter, and it was made despite the fact that he had not asked for such guidance but had simply acquiesced in what they proposed to do. By focusing their attention on helping Graham to perform penetrative sexual acts with his girlfriend, the staff are in danger of foisting on him their views of what is important about human sexuality. Rather than supporting him in developing his relationship with Kate and simply remaining sensitive to the possibility that at some point it may prove necessary to help him to come to understand something about his sexuality and about sexual relationships, they are giving Graham something more like anatomical and technical guidance about activities in which he may as yet have no real interest. Graham's story demonstrates the fact that in itself the presence of a liberal commitment to dealing positively and in life enhancing ways with the issues raised by sexuality offers no guarantee that those who are in a position to help will do what is best, or even what is helpful. Indeed in relation to Graham it might be argued that in spite of their enthusiasm and ideological commitment to helping him to lead as normal a life as possible, those who have engaged in his programme with him are likely to harm rather than enhance his development as a person with a rounded and healthy view of sex and its function in relationships.

The conservative and liberal positions revisited

Like everyone who cares for and about people with learning difficulties, most of the parents and care staff in the stories we have discussed want to do what's best for those with whom they live and work. We say this in spite of the fact that we do not believe, even in the case of those whose motives are purely directed towards the welfare of the person or persons for whom they have responsibility, some of them have done or are actually doing what is best. Their actions represent a range not only of ways of responding to sex and sexuality but of the beliefs and values that are held both by families and by professionals.

It could be argued, with some force, that this book has been written from a liberal point of view. In the introduction we have argued that to deny a person's sexuality is to treat her as less fully a person; and we believe this to be true. However, this belief does not lead straightforwardly to easy decisions about what we should do when faced with the problem of responding to the sexuality of people with learning difficulties. Although we are generally in favour of parents and care staff doing what they can to support people with learning difficulties as sexual beings, it would be simplistic to conclude from this that we believe that recognising and responding to these needs will necessarily lead to actions that will be in the best interests of those they are caring for or working with. Indeed, we have demonstrated that there is no simple correlation between liberalism and positive outcomes for users.

The extent to which positive liberal intentions have been translated into truly helpful acts of support in the stories we have discussed has varied from the consistent, ongoing and positively helpful support and encouragement received by Mr and Mrs Park, to the 'consciousness raising' and the pressure to perform imposed on Graham. Indeed, Graham's story might be considered as an example of a situation in which actions intended in good faith to help, actually amount to what could be considered a *brutal intrusion* on his life. However well meaning the intentions of the staff involved in his 'sex education' programme, their ideological commitment to the notion that he deserves the opportunity to have a normal sexual life has led to a situation in which sexual behaviours are not simply being put up with, or even encouraged, but are actually being imposed upon him. We have also seen that the adoption of a conservative stance can lead to negative results, however well intentioned the care staff and family members involved. So, for example, in several of the stories, parents who were anxious to keep their child from harm and at the same time to encourage them to develop adult interests, contrived to deflect them from anything other than the most mundane adult activities and restrictive adult company with people outside their peer group. And the way in which the residential care staff in Shirley's home restricted her relationship with Patrick, however much their actions in doing so adhered to the letter of the law and perhaps agency policy, was an affront to this couple's right to privacy which, if not leading to obviously harmful effects, certainly did nothing positive to enhance their lives.

Sexual rights: benefits and risks

We have argued that the sexuality of people with learning difficulties should be recognised and respected as part of their wholeness as human persons. Given this we must face up to the question of how we are to do so. For example, how are we to offer opportunities for sexual expression while at the same time ensuring that people with learning difficulties do not run unnecessary or unacceptable risks?

Do people with learning difficulties have rights in the area of sexuality?

One response to the need for staff and the public to be able to deal with the difficult tasks of weighing up rights, risks and responsibilities has been to make declarations about the sexual rights of people with learning difficulties (see, for example, Craft, 1983). The principles of normalisation have been influential in the production within social work and health settings of a number of lists of such 'rights'. We do not propose to offer detailed discussions of lists of rights put forward by other authors or by people with whom we have spoken. Rather we intend to state as simply as possible those 'rights' that we think could reasonably be claimed by, or on behalf of, this group of citizens, as a way of drawing attention to their needs. With this in mind we offer the following for consideration:

● The right to be informed about sexuality and its place in human life, at times and at a level that allows this area of human being and experience to be as positive as possible.

- The same right as everyone else to enjoy sexual activity. The concomitant right to remain celibate and to refrain from sexual activity of any kind.

- The right to contraceptive advice and services both to avoid pregnancy and to avoid the risks of sexually transmitted diseases.

- The same right as any other citizen to marry or form ongoing sexual relationships.

- The same right to choose parenthood that is enjoyed by everyone else.

- The right not to be sexually abused and to be protected from sexual abuse.

Let us say a little about each of these possible and proposed 'rights' in turn.

The right to be informed about sexuality and its place in human life, at times and at a level that allows this area of human being and experience to be as positive as possible

Some people might think this statement rather bland, somewhat lacking in focus. They might, for example, consider that a statement about the rights of people with learning difficulties to be informed about sex and sexuality should be more specific about the knowledge that they have a 'right' to receive. They might prefer a statement that was explicit about the right for people with learning difficulties to know about their bodies and emotions and that made recommendations about the depth and volume of such knowledge. In our view, it is inappropriate to lay down a detailed syllabus for knowledge of sex and sexuality as part of a person's entitlement to be informed. Those who are charged with the care and education of people with learning difficulties will be best placed to assess what an individual is ready to assimilate and use, and what it is necessary for them to know at each stage; and they will thus have to tailor the way in which knowledge is passed on and when, in negotiation with the individual concerned and, where appropriate, their family.

The same right as everyone else to enjoy sexual activity. The concomitant right to remain celibate and to refrain from sexual activity of any kind

While agreeing in principle with the idea implied by this statement that people with learning difficulties should have the right to enjoy sex, many would again think that our way of stating this right is somewhat bland, perhaps even rather coy. After all, we do not spell out in any detail just what sexual activities people with learning difficulties are to be given the right to engage in and enjoy. No apology is offered for this because we do not think that it is any part of our business to offer a menu for sexual enjoyment for anyone else. It is important to note that we have been careful in the wording chosen for this statement, because we are wary of the possibility that anyone should develop the idea that whereas people with learning difficulties should have the right to enjoy sex this enjoyment is to be limited in some way by what we, or someone else, believes is proper for them. Indeed, other than socially determined taboos about sexual activities that may be harmful to the participants or others, we cannot even begin to imagine how anyone could make a decision about what it is proper for others to enjoy sexually. It is also important to note that we have chosen to talk in terms of the right to 'enjoy sexual activity' rather than 'to enjoy sexual relationships' because we recognise that sexual enjoyment can result from solo activities as well as from activities involving a partner.

In contrast to our statement about the right of people with learning difficulties 'to enjoy sexual activity', some statements of proposed rights in the area of sexuality include a reference to 'the right to enjoy loving relationships'. This only makes sense on the assumption that anyone with whom the individual in question has the right to enjoy a loving relationship (and here we assume that the loving relationships in question are sexual in nature, whether or not they issue in physical acts) is a willing partner in that loving relationship. It certainly could not be the case that just because she had learning difficulties a person had the right to a loving relationship with another unless the subject of her love felt the same way about her.

It is also worth reflecting on the fact that statements covering broadly the same purpose are sometimes phrased in terms that could exclude the right of a person to 'loving relationships' with a person of the same sex. Consider for example, the statement that Craft (1983) includes in her list: 'The right to enjoy love and to be loved by the opposite sex, including sexual fulfilment.'(p2) Statements of this kind could be seen as discriminating against people with learning difficulties whose sexual orientation is homosexual rather than heterosexual. This suggests a failure to consider the possibility that people with learning difficulties might enjoy sexual relationships with people of the same sex and this, to our minds, would be not only mistaken but unjust. Of course, a person who believes that people with learning difficulties have a right to have loving sexual relationships with people of the opposite sex, but not with people of the same sex, might also believe that loving same-sex relationships between regular people are not to be covered by a statement of rights.

This would have the merit that it was consistent, though to our minds that would not make it any more just.

It is important to make plain our reasons for suggesting that the right of people with a learning disability to enjoy sexual activity is the same as that enjoyed 'by everyone else.'

First, we consider that restrictions that apply to other people should also apply to people with learning disabilities. For example, we do not consider that a person with learning difficulties, more than any other person, should have a right to engage in sexual activities in places that offend other people. Nor do we consider that by virtue of having learning difficulties a person should have the right to enjoy sexual activities that involve abusing other people, or to engage in taboo sexual activities.

Second, it is important to stress that we do not believe that people with learning difficulties have any more right than anyone else to have their sexual needs provided for. We must distinguish between the idea that it is right to treat people with learning difficulties in respectful ways that recognise them as sexual beings and the notion that this means that they have a right to sex and a sex life. In other words, although an individual may have the right to be free from constraints on her own behaviour provided that it causes no injury to others, she does not have the right to expect that she will be provided with the equipment, persons and opportunities that will allow her to be sexually satisfied.

Moral qualms about the provision of sex by paid employees aside, in an ideal world an argument might be made in favour of sex being provided by some agency of the welfare state; after all, a happy and fulfilled sex life is one factor in determining the overall state of wellbeing of people. Though this is true, however, it should be noted that similar arguments could be made in favour of the provision of many other aspects of human life that can help us to flourish. For example, such an argument might be made in favour of the provision of Mediterranean cruises, decent housing, proper jobs, proper health and dental care, and adequate and efficient transport; and perhaps the provision of sex cannot compete with these in the eyes of those within the government who decide on the allocation of money. It should also be noted that even if sex could be provided out of the public purse, a separate argument would be needed to justify its differential provision for specific groups such as those with learning difficulties, even though there might be good grounds on which such an argument might be constructed.

Finally, we must distinguish between the idea that people with learning difficulties have a right to enjoy sexual activities and the idea that they must engage in them. This is why we have added the second part of this statement, referring to the right to remain celibate and to refrain from sexual activity of any kind. Although it might seem hardly necessary to spell this out, we have done so because we are conscious of the danger that over-enthusiastic liberalism could lead unthinking if caring professionals to act in ways that are similar to the staff of Graham's social education centre.

The right to contraceptive advice and services both to avoid
pregnancy and to avoid the risks of sexually transmitted diseases

Related to the idea that people with learning difficulties should have a right to contraceptive services is the idea that in those countries where women have a legal right to abortion as a means of avoiding parenthood this should be a right shared by women with learning difficulties. We shall thus deal with the supposed right to abortion along with the proposed right to contraception.

It is difficult to say how far the supposed right to contraceptive advice should extend. For example, should it extend to all people? Or should restrictions be placed on it depending on the country in question? And should it be granted only to people over a certain age – the age at which the right to have sexual intercourse is granted? Certainly in countries that are predominantly Catholic there will be no legal right to contraception, and in most countries there will be restrictions on the age at which people are entitled to engage in sexual intercourse. We do not want to enter deeply into a discussion of these questions, though they do suggest the need for reflection about the nature of such 'rights' and, indeed, about the nature of rights in general; about, for example, whether it can make sense to talk about rights that are universal to all people or whether, rather, they are restricted in application to particular places and particular times.

Sometimes statements relating to the right of people with learning difficulties to receive contraceptive help, draw attention to the fact that they may have contraceptive needs that are different from those of other people, by adding that the services should be 'specialised to meet their needs' (see for example, Craft, 1983, who refers to 'birth control' rather than contraception). In reality, this frequently implies the use of contraceptive medication, often of a long-acting kind, in order to avoid women with learning difficulties becoming pregnant. Many ethical issues are raised by the use of contraceptive medication as a long term solution to the perceived risk that women with learning difficulties might become pregnant; amongst these are issues relating to the increased dangers of medical conditions and long term fertility problems that are attendant on the use of such medication. Others arise from the way that certain stereotypical images of women with learning difficulties underpin decisions about the appropriateness of contraceptively 'protecting' them, including the idea that they might be promiscuous or open to abuse. In relation to these points, it is worth noting that since what is aimed at is avoiding the possibility of pregnancy as a result of sexual intercourse it would be more appropriate and more ethical to do so by educating women about the hazards of both abuse and promiscuity and, where appropriate, by supervising them closely enough to ensure that they do not unwillingly or unwittingly become pregnant.

Although contraceptive measures can to some extent protect a person from some of these hazards – for example, from disease and from the possibility of becoming pregnant or of making someone else pregnant – they cannot eliminate them altogether. Nor can they do anything at all to protect a person from the risk of abuse or from the other risks that come with a promiscuous life style. In any case, contraceptive measures can only offer protection against this limited range of risks if the methods adopted are suitable and they are used efficiently and effectively; the use of the contraceptive pill, for example, can do nothing to combat the risk of catching sexually transmitted diseases, nor can it protect against pregnancy if it is used irregularly. And barrier methods of contraception can only protect against sexually transmitted diseases if they are used correctly.

It seems important to assert our belief that, even if it is valid, the idea that a person with learning difficulties has a right to contraceptive services, and perhaps to abortion, must not be construed in a way that suggests that it is always right to impose such measures on the person in question because others believe that it is necessary to do so. In relation to the idea that women with learning difficulties have the same right as other women to termination of pregnancy, it is difficult to envisage any circumstances in which it might be justified to impose an abortion on a woman with learning difficulties who did not wish to have one. However, we are well aware that in the not too distant past this procedure and others such as sterilisation, whilst being described as 'voluntary', have in fact been imposed on women with learning difficulties by professionals and parents who believed, for example, that pregnancy itself might be too difficult and upsetting for such women and who considered this to be sufficient cause to override the woman's views.

The same right as any other citizen to marry or form ongoing sexual relationships

Though we believe that people with learning difficulties have the right to form ongoing sexual relationships and marry, it is important to note that this does not mean that we believe that they have the right to form such relationships with or marry whomsoever they wish. It could not be the case that anyone had the right to marry unless the person they wanted to marry also wished to marry them; and the same is true of the right to form ongoing sexual relationships. This is just as true of people with learning difficulties as it is of anyone else; that is why we have modified this statement by again adding the caveat about the right to marry and form such relationships being the same as that of 'any other citizen'.

The same right to choose parenthood that is enjoyed by everyone else

In Part Four we address, in some detail, the question of whether people with learning difficulties should be permitted to become parents, and so in a sense we are jumping the gun here. We believe that if anyone has a right to choose parenthood then this is a right that all people share, including those with learning difficulties. Concomitant with this right is the same right to choose against parenthood that any other citizen holds, which implies the right, in a country where abortion is readily available, for women with learning difficulties to terminate a pregnancy.

It is important to be clear about our belief that any limitation of the choice in favour of parenthood should not depend upon the question of whether the prospective parent is ordinary in intellectual terms or has learning disabilities. This is just as true in relation to the creation of families by artifical means as it is in relation to families that are naturally created. Countless ordinary prospective parents are denied the possibility of parenthood by any of the means by which families can be 'artificially created', including adoption as well as the use of the new technology of reproduction including in-vitro fertilisation (IVF), artifical insemination by a donor or the husband (AID and AIH), and surrogacy. This is not the place to discuss the rightness or wrongness of the reasons that may be given for deciding whether or not prospective parents should be admitted to programmes involving such technologically based 'treatments'. However, we should make clear our belief that people with learning disabilities should not be either privileged or discriminated against in respect of such decisions simply on the basis that they have learning disabilities.

Finally, we want to contrast our statement of a proposed right of people with learning difficulties to make decisions about becoming parents with other statements of supposed rights in the same area. It has been suggested, for example by Craft (1983), that the principles of normalisation imply that men and women with learning difficulties have

'The right to have a voice in whether or not they should have children.' (p2) We prefer to stay with the idea that if there is a right in this area it is the right to choose parenthood and not simply to create, carry and give birth to children. As will become obvious from what we say in Part Four, and without being naively romantic about the likelihood that people with any degree of learning disability can be good and successful parents, we are wary of the idea that restrictions should be placed on the right of people with learning difficulties to decide for themselves whether parenthood is for them, unless this restriction is placed on all people.

The right not to be sexually abused and to be protected from sexual abuse

When we produced our first list of proposed rights, some people queried whether we had included all of the rights in the matter of sexuality to which people with learning disabilities are entitled. In particular we were asked why we had not included the right not to be sexually abused. We had thought hard about whether we should include such a right in our list and had decided against it. Although it is clear that people with learning difficulties have such a right, it seemed to us to be so obviously the case, not only that this was so but also that this is a right in which everyone shares, that we believed that it would be not only unnecessary but unhelpful to say so. On reflection, however, we have decided to include this right and also the right to be protected from abuse. Given the nature of the society in which we live and the fact that people with learning difficulties are, in common with other disabled people, so commonly *disvalued*[1], we now believe that it is necessary to state this right, if only to acknowledge that as a society we recognise that such rights are commonly abused and that it is intolerable to us that they should be. In Part Three we outline our views about the responsibilities that the right to be free from sexual abuse lays not only on families and front line staff but also on those middle and senior managers who are engaged in reshaping services as they change from being institutional to being community based.

Rights, responsiblities and the avoidance of harm

Some people would say that people with learning difficulties do not have all of the rights in relation to sexuality that we have outlined. Although they might agree that such people have the right to contraception or abortion or, more positively, to be informed about sex and to enjoy sexual activity, they might, for example, argue that because they are incapable of sufficient self control or responsibility people with learning difficulties cannot and should not be granted rights to have loving relationships, to marry and have children. Some of those who would argue thus might do so because they do not believe that people with learning difficulties really are people like you and like us and therefore do not share in the same rights as we do.

In weighing up the balance between facilitating people with learning difficulties in their sexuality by making sure that they are knowledgeable and protected, and the tendency to discourage relationships because of potential risks, we must ask ourselves not only what we think are the principal benefits but also what we think are the principal risks. We must try to decide whether these risks outweigh the moral arguments in favour of facilitating relationships. We must ask ourselves what we can reasonably do to ensure that sexuality for people with learning disabilities does not become a destructive and negative aspect of life. In doing so we have to avoid any prescriptive and simplistic understanding of the balance between rights and responsibilities; between the right to sexual expression and the need for protection.

Not so many years ago the principal risk identified by parents, teachers and other professionals would probably have been the possibility, in the case of young women, that they might become pregnant. The advent of AIDS has made it less sensible to view the avoidance of pregnancy as the most serious worry. HIV and AIDS have made sex a potentially lethal activity for those who do not, or perhaps cannot, take care to protect themselves and others, and it is arguably the case that the principal problem has become that sex, if unprotected, penetrative and unsafe, can kill. Yet for many people, including staff, parents and the public, the primary concern remains that if a woman with learning difficulties is allowed to have a relationship with a man she will become pregnant; hence the prevalence of the view that it is morally okay to sterilise people with learning difficulties or to arrange, without their consent, that they are chemically protected against pregnancy. Underlying this concern are probably a number of unspoken prejudices and fears including the unconsidered view that people with learning difficulties are unable to cope with the tasks of parenting and the fear that if they do become parents their children will be at risk of neglect and even abuse.

Drastic steps to avoid pregnancy may also be taken on the grounds that it is in the best interests of a woman with learning disabilities that this should happen. Draper (1991) discusses 'Jeanette', a 17 year old girl in relation to whom the House of Lords agreed to a sterilisation being carried out in May 1987. Among the reasons for Jeanette's proposed sterilisation were the fact that she was unlikely to be able to understand the changes that would occur in her body were she to become pregnant, that she disliked little children and demonstrated no maternal instincts. If these things were true, and we must assume they were, there was certainly good reason for those who were charged with Jeanette's care to try to arrange that she did not become pregnant. The question of whether anyone else should have been allowed to decide against pregnancy on Jeanette's behalf need not concern us here though presumably the view of the House of Lords was that there were grounds to allow this.

What does concern us is the question of whether the best way – the most humane, life enhancing way for Jeanette to be helped to avoid pregnancy – was to carry out a serious operation on her in order to prevent conception taking place should she be impregnated by a man. Here we agree with Draper who points out that 'sterilisation is not a substitute for adequate care'. (p96) In other words, we believe that in relation to Jeanette and other similar women a better course of action would be to take good enough care of the woman in question to avoid situations coming about where she will be at risk of abuse from men and in which she is placed in a situation where, by promiscuous behaviour, she is open to the risk of pregnancy, among other risks[2]. In recent years the possibility of sexual abuse of people with learning disabilities has perhaps become as important a fear as the possibility of pregnancy. As a result, it is perhaps paradoxical that measures designed to protect young women from pregnancy probably lay those who are thus 'protected' open to an increased risk of abuse by making the detection of abuse less likely.

Facilitating the sexual development of people with learning difficulties could, at its most life enhancing and most positive, be seen as an invitation to all kinds of pleasure; on the other hand it could, at its most negative, be viewed as an invitation to all kinds of danger. So how do we arrange that people with learning difficulties, whose sexual nature we want to respect and who we may want to support or even encourage in their sexuality, do not engage in activities that put them in mortal danger? Well, of course, we can't arrange this. We can educate and we can guard and we can take care, but we cannot entirely avoid the possibility that a sexually active person may enter into activities that are dangerous for him or her. But then we cannot do this for anyone with sexual feelings and needs. Nevertheless, the dangers that lurk in the positive nature of sexuality must be taken into account by those who would argue in favour of facilitating people with learning difficulties in this area. Vigorously supporting people with learning difficulties in the development of their sexual lives carries risks that we cannot avoid. Apart from the risks of unwanted pregnancy and disease, there is the risk of abusive relationships, and in Part Three we discuss a number of stories about people with learning difficulties, living independent and semi-independent lives in the community, who fall prey to unscrupulous men and women whose sole interest is in their own sexual gratification.

Focusing on danger, whether from strangers or from disease and the possibility of pregnancy, is to fail to take account of what others might consider to be the main cause for concern. This is the possibility (even the likelihood) of relationships breaking down – and the emotional trauma that this is likely to cause. It is a cliché, but probably true nonetheless, that most people who have engaged in close friendships which have broken down have, at some time, suffered trauma as a result; when relationships are sexual, this trauma is likely to be even greater. The traumatic effect will be no different whether the person who is let down has, or does not have, learning difficulties.

Of course, in the case of those who are commonly thought, even by practitioners who should know better, not to have sexual feelings (or who it is thought should not have them), emotional trauma following the breakdown of a relationship may be missed or even misinterpreted. We know of a couple, both of whom had Down's syndrome and learning difficulties, who met in a large institution, settled down together and were eventually happily married and lived in their own home for some years. When, as is all too common in marriage, this couple encountered difficulties in their relationship and parted company, the support services seemed to find it impossible to believe that the man's distress following the breakdown of his marriage was the result of losing his partner, his wife, his lover, his 'other half', and chose instead to interpret it as the onset of pre-senile dementia. This story demonstrates that close relationships of an emotional, intellectual and physical kind, in other words relationships between two people in their wholeness as people, can be not only a source of joy but a source of sorrow and devastation for people with learning difficulties just as much as it can for their regular peers. And yet the emotional problems that may result from the formation of sexual relationships are much less likely to concern those who care for people with learning difficulties than the practical problems to which we have already referred.

Denying the sexuality of people with learning difficulties

We have suggested that there is a continuum of views about the fact that people with learning difficulties are just the same as everyone else in having a sexual nature. At one end of this continuum is the will to embrace and celebrate their sexuality which, combined with the desire to do right and the duty to care, can lead to a range of interventions aimed at assisting people with learning difficulties to adjust to, grow in, and enjoy their sexuality – though we pointed out that not all these interventions will be helpful. At the other end of the continuum is the desire to sublimate the sexuality of people with learning difficulties, to deflect it, or otherwise ignore it. We have discussed some possible rights that people with learning difficulties may be said to have, in relation to sexuality. We want now to focus attention on some of the ways in which the sexuality of people with learning difficulties may be denied, beginning with, and paying particular attention to, the ways in which such denial may occur at the transition to adulthood that comes with puberty and adolescence.

Physically, adolescents have moved or are moving through puberty; they are becoming sexually aware and often sexually active. Knowledge of sex, whether it is well founded or picked up in the playground, youth club or pub, is, for adolescents, the kind of knowledge that is worth having. And it is at a premium; as Measor (1989) points out, there is status to be won or lost in the possession of knowledge about sexual matters since, 'One rule of adolescent culture is that you must always pretend to know everything; you cannot admit ignorance about any sexual matter.' (p. 42)

Sex education is now part of the accepted curriculum of most schools. In spite of this, it is paradoxically the case that the task of learning about sex is often one of the most difficult for adolescents, and they still probably pick up most of their sexual knowledge from friends and from illicit viewing of movies to which they do not legally have access in a cinema, rather than from their parents or other responsible adults. As a result of the knowledge that they either have or pretend to have, combined with their physical maturation, many regular adolescents will set out on what for them, even in the age of AIDS, is an exciting adventure. However, what for them constitutes an adventure will often, for their parents, constitute a worry on a nightmarish scale.

Although physically, as they move through puberty, young people with learning difficulties look more and more like young adults, in some ways they may not be ready to assimilate either the changes that are occurring in their bodies or in the expectations that others might have of them. They are less likely than their regular peers to move away from their parents, to become more independent and more involved with their peer group; their reliance on their parents is less likely to diminish. Given this, it is hardly surprising that at times people with learning difficulties need special help in progressing through the normal processes of adolescence, without which they may end up being dependent on others for ever.

Many parents of young people with learning difficulties will respond sensitively to their youngster's developing physical and psychological maturity in order both to protect and educate them as they approach and grow through adolescence. Others are less likely to do what's right even though their motivation is just as altruistic. For example, it is common, and to some extent understandable, for parents of people with learning difficulties to fail to adjust their expectations of their child as he or she matures; to some extent they share this with many typical parents. Often this will happen as the result of fears about how their child can cope with adult life. However, some reasons for such failure to adjust may relate not to the parents' beliefs and fears about the youngsters themselves but to subconscious concerns about their own needs. Baker (1991) cites Card, who suggests a number of reasons parents might have for encouraging continued dependency, including the desire to avoid the pain and loss involved in the separation of their son or daughter from the family, the financial advantages of having them at home, and the loss of a focus for family activity. Viewing the problem in this way might lead us to think in terms of the dependency of the parents on their youngster rather than the reverse. Consider, for example, the following stories in which young men at different stages in their lives look destined to remain closely attached to their parents, because their parents have failed, or are failing, to help them to grow up towards independence.

> Mr and Mrs Jones were very pleased when their son Peter arrived years after they had given up hope of becoming parents. As a result they have always looked on him as their 'special blessing'. And since they realised that he wasn't quite like other children, they have looked on his care as their special task in life. Well, these things (having children who are a bit different) often happen with children born to older parents, don't they? Still they've done their best to bring him up to live as normal a life as he could hope to have, though they always realised that he could never live independently. That is why, now that they are getting old, they are concerned about the future; about who will look after him when they have gone. And sex? Well of course sex isn't in it as far as Peter goes. Though he is now 28, he is like a little boy, their little boy, and all that is beyond him.

Peter's parents have engaged in what we might think of as a process of *developmental suspension*. They have kept Peter, like his namesake in the Barrie story (Barrie, 1911), as a little boy, long after he ceased, biologically, to be one. What is more, they have encouraged others to view him as a boy rather than as a man, by their choice of clothes for him. Though there may well be a financial advantage for Peter's parents, and others like them, in keeping their 'grown-up child' at home, we do not doubt that they want what is best for him. Their reason for tying him to the home is not the thought of financial advantage. It is likely that their motives relate to subconscious concerns about their own needs, including the need not to disturb established and comfortable ways of relating to one another as a family.

Brian's parents are nearing retirement age. He has always needed constant supervision and his parents receive both day and night attendance allowance. Though, as his parents say, he is a 'good boy', he has always been a bit of a handful and once a month he spends a weekend with a link family in order to give his parents and sisters a bit of a rest. Brian attends school five days a week and is in the leaver's group there. Next year it is expected that he will go on to the day centre, with day release to attend a life skills class at the town library.

Brian has a number of interests including music and snooker. He enjoys helping his mum in the kitchen, but his greatest strength as far as his parents are concerned is that he loves working in the garden and he is a great help to his dad, who is beginning to find heavy jobs like mowing the lawn a bit of an effort. His parents have never contemplated the possibility that Brian will ever live independently. After all, though he is a big lad and able to help about the home, he will never really be able to manage on his own. This is one reason they have discouraged his friendship with Freda; another is that they don't want him to suffer distress when he leaves school, because Freda will be going on to the FE College and they will probably never see one another again.

Brian's parents may simply be concerned about his well-being and his inability to cope with certain aspects of everyday living. On the other hand, they may also be concerned about their own needs; indeed at an implicit or subconscious level their needs might be more important, because if Brian should leave them they would lose an unpaid helper and someone who contributes to the family income.

Peter's parents have failed to realise that their son is no longer their little boy. As a result, they have failed to foster his possibilities for independence; and in doing so they may well have set up their nightmare scenario – one in which, after they die, he will not only have no-one to look after him but will be unable to look after himself and will thus have to be cared for by strangers, away from his home, wherever a place can be found for him. With help, Peter could still develop skills in independent living that would allow him to care for himself in the future; however it is unlikely now that his parents can be persuaded to let go enough for this to happen. In contrast to Peter, Brian still has the chance of growing up and becoming an independent adult. He has yet to leave school, and when he goes to the day centre and begins his course at the library he could easily develop the skills he needs for independent living. But this will only work out if his parents can be helped to see that it would be in his best interests. And like many other parents of young people with learning difficulties, Brian's parents seem to have a vested interest in keeping him at home with them.

There is nothing specific in the stories of Peter and Brian to suggest that their parents' ways of thinking about these young men draw on concerns about sex, or even that their parents have given a great deal of thought to questions about growing up at all. Yet both have gone through puberty and have developed the physical features that distinguish them as men rather than boys, despite the fact that, even at the age of 28, Peter's parents still choose to dress him in clothes that are inappropriate for a man of his age.

Despite the changes that are occurring in the bodies and in the emotions of people with learning difficulties who are growing through adolescence, their parents might be unwilling or unable to change their expectations and as a result might deny such changes. There are two main reasons why this might happen. First, it might result from a desire on the part of some parents or service providers to maintain their youngsters in a position of eternal childhood; and second, it might result from the not uncommon tendency in some service settings to over-emphasise adulthood and adult status at the expense of the period and process of transition that is adolescence. Such denial is not necessarily deliberate; for the best of reasons, many, perhaps most, will act unthinkingly in ways that involve or amount to denial in an attempt to do what they believe to be right for the young person in question. Other parents may have fears so great that they find it difficult to express consciously the overwhelming risks they believe their child may face if she/he is allowed more freedom.

Consider, for example, Jane Stafford who we discussed earlier and whose parents refused to allow her to take part in sex education classes at college. Like all parents, the Staffords were worried about the risks their daughter would have to face as she grew up. Their reason for refusing to allow Jane to participate in sex education was to do with their wish to protect her from possible harm, although others might have viewed their refusal as tantamount to putting Jane's head in the sand as well as their own. But far from protecting her from harm it could be argued forcefully that by denying Jane access to knowledge Mr and Mrs Stafford actually increased the possibility of harm, because leaving her in ignorance meant that she was not equipped even to begin making informed choices and decisions about this area of her life. Worse than that, by denying her the possibility of acquiring the knowledge necessary both to make informed decisions and to protect herself, Jane's parents may have put her at greater risk in the outside world where those who would sexually misuse and abuse others can take advantage of innocence and ignorance.

The idea that the attempt to protect a young person by keeping her in ignorance might do just the opposite is worrying and possibly contentious; after all, those who seek to protect their young people in this way are likely to keep just the kind of close watch over their whereabouts and actions that some of the parents we have discussed did. But it is never possible to keep a 24 hour watch over another person, especially when they spend part of their time elsewhere – for example, at school or at a social education centre. In Part Three we discuss stories in which people with learning difficulties have been abused in such contexts by the very people who have been entrusted with their care. More contentious still is the idea that some of the ways in which parents and other adults respond to the sexual changes at puberty and at adolescence, and some actions designed to protect the welfare of a person with learning difficulties in the area of sexuality, might in themselves be seen as a kind of abuse.

> Beth's mother arranged that she should have a hysterectomy in order to save her 'the messy bother of menstruation'. Some time later Beth was found to be stealing sanitary towels from her friends and smearing them with a chemical in order to simulate menstruation because, like most adolescents, she wanted to be like her friends.[3]

What are we to make of this scenario? Beth's mother alleged that the reason for the hysterectomy was to help her daughter to avoid some of the physical and emotional problems that were being caused for her by becoming a woman; but Beth herself went to great lengths to recreate the problems from which the hysterectomy was supposed to free her. Some people might wonder whether Beth's mother really acted in order to help her daughter or whether the person she intended to save bother and mess was herself. Arguably, even if her reasons for acting as she did were genuinely to do with her daughter's welfare, Beth's mother wronged her because by her actions she denied her daughter her womanhood and the right to be like her friends. Arguably also, she did her another serious wrong because, far from making abuse less likely, taking away the possibility that Beth might become pregnant could have laid her more open to abuse by removing one possible means by which abuse might be detected. At best, her mother's actions constituted a well intentioned though unsuccessful attempt to spare her daughter the practical and emotional problems associated with menstruation; at worst, they might be viewed as having arranged for medicalised physical or even sexual abuse of her daughter.

You might think that we are being a bit tough on Beth's mother because you can understand the very real desire to avoid the bother and upset of menstruation and therefore believe it plausible that she was simply attempting to avoid upset for her daughter. After all, you might argue, she did not intend to harm Beth, but to do what was best for her. This is probably true; most parents want what's best for their children. But it remains true that even if her actions were well intentioned, Beth's mother acted in a way that did not solve the problem of mess and bother that menstruating was causing. Beth did not consent to her hysterectomy, and we might take her later actions in attempting to simulate menstruation as an indication, albeit retrospective, of her refusal of consent. And since she began stealing sanitary towels and simulating menstruation in order to be like her friends, it could be argued that her mother simply substituted the problems of mess and bother by the problem of feigned menstruation perhaps paving the way for deeper identity problems.

That Beth's mother did not intend harm does not make the damage she inadvertently caused less harmful, just as the harm caused by a drunken driver is not less serious because he did not intend to kill the innocent pedestrian who died under the wheels of his car. If she was doing her best to help her, Beth's mother was not guilty of carelessly disregarding her daughter's welfare. Nevertheless she was guilty of failing fully to consider the possible implications of her actions. Even if she was well meaning and even if the results of her actions had been good for Beth, her decision to have a hysterectomy performed was made on trivial grounds and seems inappropriate; Beth had no physical problem that merited such drastic action and the procedure was carried out for reasons relating to convenience rather than health. It simply would not have been considered as an option if Beth had been a girl who did not have learning disabilities.

Whether well meaning or not, Beth's mother denied her daughter not only the ongoing experience of those aspects of womanhood that would be evidenced by her menstrual cycle, but also the possibility in the future of becoming a biological parent. Let us look now at another story in which a parent decides on a course of action that would deny her daughter's sexuality both now and in the future, though this time for reasons that are even more trivial than those that Beth's mother used to justify Beth's surgery.

Jackie had no spoken language; however, she used about a dozen Makaton signs and her receptive vocabulary was quite large. She was described as 'a very slow hyperactive'; constantly on the move, she did everything very slowly. In intellectual terms Jackie was described as being 'like a big toddler, but streetwise'. She was physically dexterous – she could, for example, undo laces and could feed and dress herself and deal with other similar self care tasks. She learned quickly when rewarded immediately.

Jackie had a number of behaviours that other people found upsetting, one of the most distressing of which was her incessant eating. She liked to feel her mouth full and what it was full of didn't seem to matter much; and so she seemed to eat constantly; and she would regurgitate what she had eaten. She would eat almost anything – newspapers, socks, carpets, or the soft parts of sofas.

Jackie's eating and regurgitation finally became too much for her parents when she began menstruating and took to eating her sanitary towels, used and unused. This caused embarrassment and distress to her family and to others, so much so that her mother was eventually advised that she should consider a hysterectomy in order to solve the problem caused by Jackie's new dietary fad.[4]

Whereas it is at least possible to imagine circumstances in which a hysterectomy might be justified as a solution to problems caused by menstruation, we cannot begin to imagine any justification for performing major surgery in order to prevent the aesthetic offence caused to others by Jackie's behaviour. Indeed, it does not seem too far fetched to think of her proposed hysterectomy as a kind of abuse. It was clearly not intended to benefit her, but others: her parents, and those who might be disgusted and embarrassed by the sight of her eating soiled sanitary towels. You might care to consider the question of whether you think it could ever be valid to perform major surgery on a person in order to prevent behaviour that is offensive to others. Our opinion is that it could not and that, as in the worst case scenario in relation to Beth's story, hysterectomy for Jackie would have amounted to medicalised sexual abuse.

Might there be situations in which hysterectomy could be justified in relation to a young woman with no gynaecological problems? Let us look at another story in which hysterectomy was proposed, not for the kind of trivial reasons that we have rejected in relation to both Beth and Jackie but for more significant reasons.

Mandy attended a mainstream school part time. She had severe learning difficulties and exhibited challenging behaviour. She was a capable student, provided she was constantly supervised on a one to one basis. However, if left unsupervised, Mandy abused herself by biting her hands and pulling her hair and as a result her hands were kept bandaged at times. In addition she was aggressive towards others, often kicking and punching them. These behaviours would have been difficult enough but Mandy also had other behaviour patterns which staff found even more difficult to deal with. In particular she frequently exposed herself. This was undignified for her and offensive to others. As a result the decision was taken that she should wear trousers rather than a skirt at school, even though standard school uniform for girls was a skirt. This decreased Mandy's exposing to some extent because of the difficulty she experienced in removing her trousers without assistance.

When Mandy started her periods she became extremely distressed and aggressive when she saw the blood. After that her challenging behaviour worsened very noticeably. She objected to having to wear sanitary towels and managed to discard them in spite of the difficulty she experienced in removing her trousers. In fact the desire to remove sanitary towels led to an increase in her exposing behaviour. Her self harming behaviour also increased during her periods and on one occasion she banged her head so hard against the wall that it was feared that she had fractured her skull. For months after this Mandy continued to experience problems at the time of her periods, and her self injuring behaviour escalated to the point at which desperate measures seemed to be called for. A case conference was held during which the possibility was raised that hysterectomy might offer a solution to the problems.

Seeing Mandy so distressed caused people in her life a good deal of pain. They had always endeavoured to make her life as normal as possible and found her self harming behaviours particularly difficult to cope with. It is easy to imagine the distress that her behaviour caused her parents and the staff at school, not to mention the other children with whom she was educated, perhaps particularly the mainstream school pupils with whom she was integrated part of the time, who may have been less used to disturbed and disturbing behaviour than those in her segregated special school.

Could the drastic step of carrying out a hysterectomy have been justified in relation to Mandy because of the very serious physical damage that she was regularly inflicting on herself? Whereas Beth's hysterectomy was carried out with the aim of making her feel better, and hysterectomy was proposed in order to prevent Jackie offending others, in relation to Mandy, it would be argued, what was at stake was her physical welfare. How could it be considered abusive, it might be asked, to do what one could to help someone about whom one cares, to overcome a problem which is now affecting all aspects of her life?

Although we do not think that early recourse to hysterectomy as a way of dealing with Mandy's challenging and self injurious behaviours would have been acceptable, we do believe that there would have been more to commend it than there was in relation to Beth. It is easy to imagine parents becoming so distraught with worry that any solution which protected their child's physical welfare could seem worthwhile, whatever the cost.

The argument in favour of surgical intervention in relation to someone like Mandy would draw attention to the real threat to her health and well being that presented itself one week in every four with monotonous regularity. Justifications for drastic treatment are sometimes given in cases where, for example, self mutilation cannot be prevented by any other method. Consider a couple of situations cited by Owens (1987, p97) in which aversive shock treatment was successfully used in order to stop self injuring behaviour; in one, a patient had bitten her own fingers so badly that amputation was necessary, and in the other a patient had chewed the flesh from his own shoulder so that bone was exposed. Owens argues that in such dire circumstances treatment of this kind may be warranted in order to prevent long term injury. We are inclined to agree that in such circumstances extreme measures may be justified if no other course of action has proved fruitful and the likelihood of success is high.

But is the risk to Mandy's life and health similar in kind and degree to the risks of serious self harm that the drastic treatments described by Owens were designed to stop?

We do not think that Mandy's story is as drastic as those described by Owens, and we do not feel inclined to believe that a hysterectomy would have been a reasonable way of dealing with the problems Mandy presented even though some aspects of her behaviour presented a risk to her health and safety. Certainly we do not think that such a measure would be reasonable until consideration had been given to a number of other possible strategies. Positive behavioural techniques can be successful in dealing with self mutilating behaviours; even better, from our point of view, would have been the implementation of a behavioural programme for Mandy combined with a more educational course of action designed to help her as far as possible to come to terms with what was happening to her body. In order to facilitate this, she could have been prescribed medication to subdue her periods for a time. Some people might object to such a use of drugs on ethical grounds, and we would have sympathy for this view if drug treatment of this kind were to be used as a long term solution. However, even the long term use of drugs would probably have been less drastic than hysterectomy.

Why is it that in the case of young women like Beth, Jackie and Mandy, and countless other girls and women with learning difficulties, there seems to be a predisposition to think that hysterectomy might be an acceptable solution to problems that are not connected to the physical health of their reproductive system, whereas we would not consider this solution to similar problems in the case of other young women who did not have learning difficulties?

By way of comparison consider Orlane and Debbie, both of whom were highly intelligent though very disturbed young women and both of whom were at times violent during their periods. Would we, realistically, condone the idea that their tendency to violence during their periods should be solved by hysterectomy? What about a teenager with anorexia nervosa whose reaction to her periods was to cease eating in order to stop them? It is highly unlikely that we would propose that she should have a hysterectomy in order to try to change the pattern of her behaviour.

One possible reason for this disparity between what might be considered permissible in relation to young women with learning disabilities and their typical peers is that as a society we do not value people with learning disabilities as highly as we do other people. This view will be offensive to many though there is evidence for its truth in the ways that society in general acts towards people who have learning disabilities. Perhaps you should consider seriously whether you agree with this view. But the most likely reason that as a society we find hysterectomy a permissible solution to the kinds of problems presented by young women like Mandy and Beth, and faced by their parents and teachers, is that we view fertility and childbearing capacity mostly in terms of the ability to found a family, and in general we do not expect or want people with learning disabilities to start families of their own.

Many people may be inclined to believe that removing the uterus of a woman with learning disabilities would not matter because, having grown up with the expectation that people with learning disabilities do not have children, they believe that there would be no harm in doing so. But, even if it were the case that most women with learning disabilities are not going to be parents, this could not justifiably be used as a reason for believing that hysterectomy is a matter of little importance in any particular instance. The effects of such procedures, and even the prospect of them, can be so distressing that many women suffer enormously as a result. Women who have faced therapeutic hysterectomy after their childbearing years often report that they have felt less of a woman because an important part of them has been taken away. There is no reason to assume, as a matter of course, that women with learning disabilities will experience this loss differently and less seriously than their regular peers.

In discussing some of the ways in which the sexuality of people with learning difficulties may be denied, we have focused on a range of possibilities, from what might be thought of as simple neglect about the fact that a young person is passing through puberty and may be developing adolescent interests, to the brutal intrusion of hysterectomy. We do not wish to suggest that anyone would wickedly mutilate youngsters with learning difficulties. However, to take such drastic action even for the best intentions lays open the possibility that the reasons behind the action may not be purely to do with doing what's best for the young person.

Let us, finally, look at a story in which it is difficult to see any possible justification for carrying out a sexually disabling procedure on a young person with a learning difficulty.

> Tom, a 'mentally handicapped' man, was sterilised at the age of twelve while in the care of an institution. By the time he was twenty two he had a job, a car, a flat and a fiancée with whom he wished to found a family, and made enquiries about the possibility of having his sterilisation reversed.

In this story a pre-emptive vasectomy is carried out on a boy who is barely pubertal. His sexuality is not so much denied as over-reacted towards in such a way that he is denied not the opportunity for a sexual life but the opportunity of parenthood. It is an example of brutal intrusion just as much as the imposition of an active sex life on Graham, to which we have already referred.

It is clear that Tom was not sterilised for his own benefit since he was not going to become pregnant. And, at the age of twelve, he was not in a position to have a stable partner in whose fertility he could take an interest. It seems most likely that, even at the age of twelve, it was anticipated that Tom was a sexual threat and that he was sterilised in order to prevent him making unsuspecting females pregnant. This presumption perhaps says something about the inclination of those who were caring for him to embrace at least some of the myths referred to at the beginning of Part Two. And even if the care staff already had evidence that Tom had a voracious sexual appetite and was liable to act to assuage this appetite by attacking women, their actions suggest that they were willing to mutilate him in the short term rather than taking better care of those women by protecting them from his potential attacks by keeping him under sufficiently close supervision and taking other action to change his behaviour. In any case, sterilising Tom does nothing to prevent him attacking women, and suggests that the staff who were caring for him were more worried by the idea of pregnancy than either the dangers of attack or the trauma that would almost certainly result.

Often people who hear Tom's story disbelieve it; they think that it is a made-up story; sometimes they simply say 'It couldn't happen here'; Tom's story is, after all, an American one. Perhaps you think this. More likely, you may have heard of similar stories – such stories are part of the living history of our institutions. Many people who hear Tom's story are appalled. They are appalled because, although they have assumed that the reason Tom was sterilised was that he was considered to be mentally handicapped, it turned out that he was quite capable of holding down a job, driving a car and much more besides. Often as a result they enter a second stage of horror when they realise the implication of their initial reaction. In short, they realise that they have accepted the idea that had Tom really been mentally handicapped it would have been accceptable to sterilise him. Generally speaking they have begun at this stage to question whether the fact that a person has a learning difficulty is grounds for treating him in ways that we would not treat those who are considered to be 'normal'. The way in which even many caring and committed people respond – thinking initially that it would have been all right to sterilise Tom if he had really been a boy with a mental handicap – gives clues about the way in which our society views those who are intellectually disabled. The disvaluing to which they are subjected seems to be part of the general ethos our society has embraced in relation to disabled people, who are devalued and treated in ways that we would not tolerate in relation to those who do not have disabilities.

Being and becoming sexual

In Part Two we have examined the ways in which, as a society and as individuals, we accept or deny the sexuality of people with learning disabilities. We have looked at a variety of ways in which both parents and professionals respond to them as sexual beings and at the fact that good intentions, whether conservative or liberal, offer no guarantee that they will do what is best for the person concerned. We have considered a variety of proposed rights in the area of sexuality and looked at the benefits and risks that facilitating people with learning disabilities in their sexuality can bring. Finally, in thinking about the ways in which the sexuality of people with learning disabilities might be denied, we found ourselves looking closely at some stories in which, as a way of solving a variety of problems, the sexuality of people with learning disabilities has been simply and somewhat starkly denied by what might be thought of as brutal intrusion into their bodies. The fact that the problems that were or could be solved by the procedures we discussed were problems faced by someone other than the sterilised person, or the person proposed for sterilisation, has led us in some instances to pose the question of whether these procedures might be viewed as abuse of a medicalised and sexual kind. In Part Three we again talk about the sexual abuse of people with learning disabilities, though we will then be addressing abuse in its more usual sense to refer to occasions when, without regard for the person with learning disabilities as a person, he or she is forced either to have sex, or to watch sex, or is otherwise used as the means to someone else's sexual gratification.

Notes

[1] By 'disvaluing' we mean devaluing to the extent that value is stripped away altogether.

[2] Presumably a woman who is unable on her own behalf to to make a decision in favour of sterilisation would also be unable to consent to having sex with a man, and therefore any sex she had (however promiscuous it looked to others) would, from her point of view at any rate, be abusive. The question of whether, from the point of view of any man who had sex with such a woman, the sex would amount to abuse, would depend, as we make clear in Part Three, on his level of understanding of the situation so that, whereas by having sex with her an ordinary man would most likely be abusing a woman like this, a man who himself had severe learning disabilities might not be doing so.

[3] This case comes from Lucy Crain (1980). She also discusses the case of the young man we call Tom, whose story is cited later in Part Two. Both were drawn to our attention by Heather Draper, who has also written about them (Draper, 1991).

[4] Jackie's story is a real one. Though her mother accepted the medical advice that she was given, to allow a hysterectomy to be carried out on her daughter, the surgery was never completed because social workers involved in the case took legal action to prevent it. Behavioural treatment was then successfully used to modify Jackie's eating habits so that they were less offensive to others.

PART THREE

Exploitation, abuse and assault: the sexual misuse of people with learning difficulties

Despite the claim that 1992 was the year in which it was finally recognised to be a widespread problem, much had already been written and spoken about the sexual abuse of people with learning difficulties[1]. Over the past few years more and more articles on the topic have appeared both in professional journals and magazines such as *Community Care, Mental Handicap* and *Community Living,* and in the national press. It has also been addressed through the other media – in both documentary and drama productions on television, for example. Thinking has drawn substantially on related areas such as the sexual abuse of children, in relation to which much work had already been carried out.

When it was initially realised that first the physical abuse and then the sexual abuse of children was occurring on a much wider scale than had previously been thought possible, articles in both the popular and the professional press served two main purposes. First of all they voiced general deprecation and horror that anyone should abuse children like this, often drawing attention to particular incidents and, where abuse occurred within child care services, to particular institutional settings in which abuse had occurred. Secondly, they contributed to the discussion not only of possible courses of action – changes to practice and so on – but also to the problems of definition and identification that underpin such practice: what was to count as abuse? how was it to be spotted?

Now that it has been recognised or discovered or admitted that the sexual abuse of people with learning difficulties is widepread, there has also been much reporting of particular incidents both of abuse within families and of abuse in service settings. Interestingly, whereas child sexual abuse tends to be reported most often when it is perpetrated in the home or by people with some connection to the home, the sexual abuse of people with learning difficulties is more commonly associated with institutional and service settings. Along with the reporting of particular incidents has come a rush of published material exploring both the conceptual and the practical problems that are raised. There is thus a body of literature about the sexual abuse of people with learning difficulties based both on research and on personal and professional experience and reflection.

We do not intend to offer a critique of the received wisdom about the sexual abuse of people with learning difficulties. Nor do we intend to offer a comprehensive overview either of research in the area, or of the opinions of those who believe that they understand the phenomenon of sexual abuse sufficiently well to be able to offer procedural guidance about what must be done to combat the practical problems that it presents. Rather we want to make some observations about the ethical issues that the sexual abuse of people with learning difficulties throws up if we take it seriously.

That people who have learning difficulties should be sexually abused, most often by people known to them and often by those charged with their care, is appalling and perhaps an indicator of sickness in our society rather than simply of the wickedness of individuals. Wounding though it is to admit, we live in a society where people with disabilities are not valued. This fact, combined with the corrupting influence of power, suggests one explanatory mechanism for the occurrence of sexual abuse perpetrated against people with learning difficulties who are less likely otherwise to be viewed as sexually desirable by most abusers. Women are abused much more frequently than men but neither age nor level of disability is a determinant of who shall and who shall not escape abuse, since victims come in all ages and all levels of intellectual ability. Abusers are most often men and most of those who abuse, abuse more than one person; abuse is rarely isolated and often happens in the context of an ongoing abusive relationship, sometimes over many years, which suggests that many abusers view their victim or victims as a long term resource rather than as people to be related to, cared for, cherished and respected.

The sexual abuse of one person by another is morally wrong, whether it takes any of the direct and physical forms that are usually collectively referred to as *contact abuse*, or any of the variety of non-direct and non-physical forms that are usually referred to as *non-contact abuse*. It is perhaps the fact that the person who is abused is relatively powerless when compared with his abuser that makes the sexual abuse of people with learning difficulties, and other vulnerable members of society such as children and elderly people, particularly morally offensive. However, the ethical issues raised by sexual abuse are complex and relate to the inability and sometimes, and in our opinion more seriously, to the unwillingness of family members or professional carers to act in relation to suspected and even actual abuse. In other words, sexual abuse raises ethical issues at a variety of levels relating not only to actual abuse but also to the ways in which people respond to abuse or to the possibility of abuse. Let us raise some of these issues by introducing you to stories in which abuse occurs.

When Phillipa was thirteen her mother remarried and Phillipa, who had severe learning difficulties, quickly formed a close relationship with her stepfather of whom she became very fond. When she was sixteen he began to impose sex on her.

David was in his mid-twenties and lived in a large mental handicap hospital. As a result both of his learning difficulties and a physical disability which severely impaired his mobility, he was unable to resist being regularly raped by a number of older male patients. Staff on the ward were aware of what was going on, but did nothing about it.

Peter Green, a staff member in a day centre, arranged the mirrors in the changing rooms for sporting activities in such a way as to allow him to watch the men in his care showering and changing. Green's reason for wanting to watch the men in this way was the sexual gratification that he gained by doing so. However, at no time did he engage in any inappropriate physical contact with them.

Allison lived in a small village on the edge of the city where she attended a social education centre. One evening a barn dance had been organised to raise funds for a local charity; transport staffed by the usual driver had been provided for centre members. On the way home Allison was the last passenger on the bus. The driver took his vehicle to an isolated spot and raped her.

Lillian, a young woman with learning difficulties, had enough social and community living skills to 'get by'. Friends and relatives described her as 'slow', 'not very bright', 'trusting' and 'willing to please'. She was in the habit of going to a fairly rough bar in a city centre each Saturday evening and generally went alone because she had no real friends. After a while she developed a 'nodding acquaintance' with some other people who also frequented the bar including a group of men who used to buy her drinks. She enjoyed being the centre of attention, and one evening they invited her back to an apartment where she had sex with them. This developed into a regular event, and, if asked, Lillian would probably have said that she 'didn't mind'.

Charles, a young man with learning difficulties who lived independently with visiting support from social services, was persuaded by neighbours into renting a satellite system so that they could join him in watching late night pornographic movies. Part of their motivation was the pleasure that they got from watching Charles's excitement while watching the films.

In our discussion of the ethical issues that sexual abuse raises, we will begin by reflecting in some detail on these stories[2]. In doing so we will be trying to unpack some of the ethical questions that they raise, at times contrasting them with other stories with which there are significant overlaps. In doing so we will also be trying to throw some light on the nature of sexual abuse, a task that we shall follow up later when we consider the attempts that others have made at definition and we reflect on the problems that definition causes. In exploring the nature of sexual abuse and of what it is both to be sexually abused and to be a sexual abuser, we will address the question of whether all perpetrators of actions that would normally be considered sexual abuse are necessarily abusers, and also the question of whether all subjects of actions that would normally be considered sexually abusive are necessarily victims of abuse. These might seem to be somewhat odd questions and we should make clear at the outset that we do not intend to offer excuses for those who wickedly take advantage of others over whom they can exert power as a means to achieving their own sexual satisfaction. Nevertheless, in coming to decisions about which acts do and which acts do not amount to sexual abuse, it is necessary to consider carefully how sexual abuse should be defined, and a consideration of these questions will prove informative in the attempt to shed some light on its definition.

Sexual abuse is not a single phenomenon but may take many forms, some of which are reflected in the stories we have shared, which present a variety of situations in which people with learning difficulties have been used by others as a means to the achievement of sexual pleasure. In most there is no hint of mutuality or reciprocity and it seems clear that the people with learning difficulties were used without regard for them as people with their own needs and wishes. In most of the situations that we have described, the people with learning difficulties did not willingly engage in the acts in which they were involved, or agree to being used by others in the way that they were used. This is the case even though the perpetrators of what looks like abuse might in some instances argue that, far from being a victim, the person with a learning disability was a willing partner. For example, Phillipa's stepfather might argue that she enjoyed having sex with him just as much as he enjoyed it with her, and he might even go so far as to claim that she seduced him rather than the other way round; Charles's neighbours would no doubt claim that all they were doing was having a bit of fun with a friend; and finally, since it is clear that Lillian went with her men friends willingly and that she did so on a number of occasions, it is likely that they would protest that they did nothing wrong.

In deciding which stories to discuss we have made no attempt accurately to reflect the extent of abuse in different settings. Nor have we tried to reflect the balance between abuse by someone known to the abused person and abuse by a stranger, or the extent to which abuse is carried out by ordinary people as opposed to other people with learning difficulties. We have chosen these stories in order to illustrate the range of ethical issues that surround sexual abuse. We begin with a story of sexual abuse that occurred within a family, then move on to address abuse that has taken place in residential settings, looking at examples of abuse both by other residents and by staff. After that we look at stories in which people with learning difficulties have suffered abuse in a day care setting. Finally, we look at examples of abuse that have taken place while the person has been living in the community with support from services.

Abuse within the family

Phillipa hadn't had any sex education because her mum and natural father had wanted to protect her from that kind of thing. She had always had a very close and affectionate relationship with her dad, her 'real dad', and when he was at home she often used to cuddle up with him on the settee at night watching TV. She was devastated when he left home, so much so that her mum was very worried that Phillipa would not take to her new 'dad' when he moved in. When Phillipa seemed to get on well with him her mum was relieved. What is more, when she began to cuddle up with her stepdad like she used to do with her natural father, her mum was overjoyed. She was besotted with her new husband and so pleased that he seemed to get on well with her daughter that, far from seeing anything wrong in their closeness, she worked hard at fostering it. Perhaps this was one reason that she seems to have failed to suspect anything, even after he began having sex with his stepdaughter.

By engaging in sex with her, Phillipa's stepfather was guilty of infidelity and would have been so irrespective of whether she had learning difficulties or not; in most people's minds, even those who have engaged in extra-marital affairs themselves, this would mean that he had acted badly, if not immorally, because in behaving as he did he betrayed his partner in order to satisfy his lustful feelings towards his stepdaughter. In contrast to this, one person with whom we have discussed this story suggested that perhaps Phillipa's stepdad was less morally reprehensible than one might at first think. She raised the possibility that he might have waited until Phillipa was sixteen before beginning to have sex with her, because by doing so he hoped to escape the possibility of prosecution for child abuse, and suggested that had he reasoned along these lines, we might have judged him to be less corrupt. 'After all', she argued, 'not everyone has the same set of moral values in relation to sex, and if this man believed that having sex with his stepdaughter would be okay provided she was above the legal age of consent then perhaps he was not morally wrong in his actions, even though they might not fit with most people's idea of right and wrong.' In arguing like this our colleague also had to assume that this man had not been taking advantage of Phillipa because she had learning disabilities but rather had simply been attracted to her and waited until he thought it would be legally safe to express his feelings in action.

Perhaps if Phillipa had been an ordinary girl, we could have been persuaded to think more leniently about her stepdad's actions, in spite of our own views of the moral propriety of stepparents having sex with their children. But Phillipa was not an ordinary girl; she was a girl with learning difficulties who had grown to love and trust the man with whom she had sex, as a daughter loves and trusts a father. That is why, regardless of whether Phillipa's stepfather acted because she had learning difficulties or simply because he found himself attracted to her, we have no doubt about the moral wrongness of his actions. It is not that we believe that it is necessarily wrong for a typical person to have a sexual relationship with one who has learning disabilities. Indeed, as we argue in Part Four, there will be occasions when such relationships will be able to stand up to close moral scrutiny. Nor are we saying that because he has committed the legal offence of having sexual intercourse with a woman with a mental handicap[3] he has necessarily acted morally badly. In our opinion, the fact that Phillipa had learning difficulties makes not only a legal but a moral difference to the way in which her stepfather should be judged. Both her level of understanding of sexuality and relationships and the parent-child relationship that existed between them meant that she could not enter into an agreement to have sex with her stepdad as an autonomous and self directed person. In other words, even if at some level she agreed to do what her stepfather wanted her to do with him, Phillipa could not be considered to have agreed to it freely.

It seems likely that the fact that Phillipa had not received any sex education at school contributed to her vulnerability, because she had received no guidance about, for example, appropriate and inappropriate touching, or about the rules that govern the ways in which it is considered proper for daughters and fathers to act together. However, it would have made little difference if she had been more informed about sex and had been aware of her own sexuality. We believe that her stepfather was morally wrong because he had sex with a person with severe learning difficulties for whom he had parental responsibility. We do not intend to enter into a discussion of whether things would have been different if Phillipa had already been an adult when her stepfather came into her life, or if by the time he began to have sex with her, one of them had been living in a different place, or if the relationship between them had changed because his marriage to Phillipa's mother had broken down, although these and other possible variations of detail in this story might, for some people, make a difference.

Phillipa's mother was unaware of what was going on between her partner and her daughter. And so, although we might think her guilty of neglect to some extent, because she failed to pick up on what was going on, this is a different matter than if she had harboured suspicions but done nothing about them. Most of us would not want to think that our spouse was actively looking out for signs that we might be sexually abusing our children or stepchildren. And so provided that Phillipa had not been displaying overt signs of distress, perhaps it is unrealistic to expect that her mother should have noticed the change in her relationship with her stepfather, which may have been so subtle as to be invisible or almost invisible.

Although this was not true in Phillipa's family it is worth reflecting on the possibility that a mother might become aware that a partner – whether or not he was a legal spouse, and whether he was the natural father or 'stepdad' of her son or daughter with learning difficulties – was having sex with them. In such circumstances a mother might have practical reasons for failing to take action; she might, for example, fear that her partner will leave or become violently aggressive and possibly eject her forcibly from the family home if confronted. Nevertheless it is clear that to permit such a situation to continue unchecked is unacceptable. Perhaps it is both realistic and reasonable to consider that turning a blind eye to what was going on should be thought just as morally reprehensible as perpetration, even if, in extreme circumstances, we could empathise with those whose fear led to denial of a problem. We are as responsible for our omissions to act as we are for the results of acts in which we actively engage, and so those who allow the abuse of others to continue when they could do something to prevent it are guilty of allowing harm to come to them.

Abuse in residential settings

David was regularly raped in the mental handicap hospital in which he lived and, athough they were aware of his plight, the staff did nothing about it. It might be argued that he was doubly abused – that he was abused not only by the men who regularly penetrated his body but also by the members of staff who knew that this was going on but did nothing about it. To permit the abuse of a fellow human being to continue when one could do something to prevent it is a matter of grave ethical concern and in most circumstances would justifiably be considered as abuse. This would be the case, for example, if the staff had chosen to allow the abuse to which David was being subjected to continue because to do something about it would be inconvenient or 'too much bother'.

Perhaps, however the hospital staff charged with David's care may have failed to act for some other reason. First of all, and perhaps most seriously, they might have taken a salacious interest in what went on, deriving a perverse kind of enjoyment from it. This would have been wicked and it would certainly be justifiable to consider such interest and its consequences as abuse. A slightly less damning possibility might be that they believed or persuaded themselves to believe that what was going on between David and the others was okay because, for example, it was 'an outlet' for emotions and energies that might otherwise have been pent up and resulted in aggressive outbursts. In other words, there might have been a degree of passivity on the part of the staff because rather than viewing what was going on as serious sexual assault they might have viewed it as a natural part of life for the men of this large institution. Though thinking this might have allowed such staff to live with their inaction, it would probably have involved some degree of self deceit about the true nature of the behaviour in question.

Allowing themselves to be seduced into accepting the assaults on David as part of the ongoing sexual life of the ward would surely constitute serious neglect on the part of the staff and may perhaps justifiably be considered as constituting abuse. But there is yet another possibility – that an individual might have wanted to do something about David's plight, either because she cared for him individually or believed, whether she liked him or not, that she had a duty to do so, and yet have felt frozen because of peer pressure. We have all worked in situations where the prevailing staff culture within an institution or unit or department leads to behaviour on the part of individuals that goes against their individual conscience, and this may well have been the way things were in the hospital where David lived. Thus an individual may have failed to act because she was afraid of repercussions from senior colleagues who, for example, either did not care sufficiently to act or refrained from intervening because doing so would have 'caused more trouble than it was worth' in terms of the effects on other patients, including those whose acts were abusing David. Someone who failed to do what was best for David because she felt intimidated by a senior colleague would nevertheless be guilty of neglect. For his part, the senior colleague in question would be at least as guilty, if not more so, even if unaware of the particular situation, because his attitudes and working practices and ideology would have been influencing his staff.

Whatever the truth about attitudes on the ward where David was abused by his fellow patients, perhaps the fact that the staff knowingly allowed the vile attacks on him to continue without intervening is morally more significant than the attacks themselves, awful though they were for him. It is likely that the perpetrators of David's ongoing abuse were less aware of the moral and personal significance of their actions than the staff were, or should have been. Not only that, but institutions such as the one in which David was living have a duty to care for and protect their residents, and allowing assaults such as those that were being perpetrated against David to continue unabated is obviously unacceptable.

Raising the possibility that care staff might knowingly allow the sexual assault of one resident by another or others to go on in front of their eyes, or round a corner in another room, might seem shocking; those who work in institutional settings might be offended or upset by it. If you feel like this you may wish to reflect for a while about what you find shocking or offensive, or about what upsets you in this suggestion. Perhaps you are inclined to think that we have invented this story; that would be comforting. Unfortunately, David's story is not only true to life but *real* in that a real person really lived through the situation that we describe and real people really allowed it to happen. Or maybe you find David's story upsetting because it rings true tó life for you, reminding you of some part of your personal or professional history, of some incident or situation of which you have been aware, perhaps even one in which you have been involved, however indirectly.

Many practitioners will have been aware at times that situations similar to David's have occurred in their workplaces but, for whatever reason, have failed to act. However you react to David's story and however it impinges on your experience to date, we invite you to imagine yourself into such a situation now and consider how it would affect your life. Do you feel confident that you would do the right thing about it? Are you even sure that you know what the right thing to do would be? What factors would affect your reaction and the actions you took? If you find this difficult, reflect for a moment on the questions 'What would I want if it was me in that situation?' 'What would I want to happen if the person with learning difficulties was my daughter or son, sister or brother?'

Now consider a related but slightly different scenario. What if you began to suspect the unthinkable possibility that someone in your care was being abused not, as in David's story, by another user or users, but by one of your colleagues? Would that make a difference to how you felt and to how you would react and respond? Do you feel confident that you would, that you *could* blow the whistle? What if the colleague was your boss? Or a close friend? What if he was unpleasant and intimidating? What if you did not have direct evidence to substantiate your suspicions?

The idea that professional carers might fail to take action in relation to a colleague who was sexually abusing clients is probably even more shocking than that they should fail to take action about abuse perpetrated by other clients. Some people may be inclined to believe that the possibility that sexual abuse perpetrated by a member of staff might go unsuspected, unnoticed or unreported by his colleagues is so far fetched that we should not even be discussing it. But this does happen. Anyone who doubts that professionals caring for vulnerable people might fail to take notice of signs that a colleague might be guilty of sexual impropriety need go no further than the history of Peter Righton, which was featured in the BBC documentary series 'Inside Story' (BBC, 1994)[4]. Righton had held many important positions relating to the care of children. His reputation in child care had not been diminished by the fact that he had contributed a chapter to an academic text about paedophilia (Righton, 1981) in which he openly raised the possibility that it might not be harmful for children to have sex with adults. For example, following a statement of strong disapproval of adults who rape, pester or 'offer sexual violence' to children, he writes, 'what I contest is the assumption that children need protection from (in the sense of denial of) any kind of sexual experience with an adult, however gentle or even educative.' (p39)

'Inside Story' investigated evidence that in spite of his professional reputation and the positions of trust he had held in relation to children Righton had led a double life. He had been active in the *Paedophile Information Exchange* and associated openly with many people known to have been implicated in the sexual misuse and/or abuse of children. For two of these Righton wrote references in connection with applications for school teaching positions in Britain, in spite of the fact that one had a conviction for 'lewd, indecent and libidinous behaviour' and the other several convictions for ' indecent assault'.

Righton's professional position and reputation seem to have helped him to avoid others becoming aware of his sexual interest in young boys, or perhaps to avoid the possibility that others would allow themselves to become aware of it. No-one who came in contact with him seems to have suspected, or allowed themselves to suspect, his true nature, though with hindsight some seem to recognise that there were signs that should have alerted them to the truth. For example, looking back during the 'Inside Story' documentary, Barbara Kahan, Director of the National Children's Bureau, feels that perhaps she 'should have made the connections earlier', and admits that Righton 'conned a wide range of people in the social work world.' (BBC, 1994). It is possible that those who work within services for people with learning difficulties are less gullible and have more insight than Righton's colleagues but this seems improbable to us.

How could it be possible for caring people to fail to report their suspicions that sexual abuse of clients, whether by other clients or by members of staff, was going on, even in the face of emerging evidence? One reason might be that embarrassment makes them unable to discuss or deal with it. The fact that embarrassment is a common reaction to sexual abuse is in part supported by the findings of Allington's study 'Sexual Abuse within Services for People with Learning Disabilities', in which staff awareness of such issues is discussed (Allington, 1992). Embarrassment is a powerful shaper of conduct and relationships and could be so extreme that a person faced with evidence that with hindsight seemed overwhelming might find herself unable even to allow her suspicions to form properly, so that they remained just on the edges of consciousness rather than coming into full focus.

If you find it difficult to contemplate the possibility that a person could fail to report suspicions about another person's conduct, consider the following group of related stories in one of which a person who has good reason for suspecting someone she knows of evil doing fails to report her suspicions:

> A parent (let's call him Parent A) who does not like his small child, takes her for a walk along the canal path. Looking carefully round to ensure that no one is within earshot, he drops the child into the canal. She cannot swim and drowns.

It seems perfectly clear that Parent A has done something wrong. He set out to harm his child and succeeded in doing so. But now consider another parent:

> Parent B is walking down the canal path with her small child, who has always been a source of anxiety and pain and has brought her little pleasure. Her child, running some way ahead, trips and falls into the water; Parent B, seeing this, begins to run forward to save him but stops. As the cries fade out and her child's head disappears below the surface, she turns for home.

Was Parent B less culpable than Parent A? We do not think so. She did not put her child in the water like Parent A. However, she did deliberately refrain from saving him; and what's more, she did so because she was glad to have him dead. Finally consider the following:

A neighbour of Parent B who spotted her in the distance, walking along the canal with her child, was hurrying along to pass the time of day when the incident we have discussed took place. Seeing Parent B hurrying to save her child then turning and walking away, she could not believe her eyes and hurried along to do what she could to help. By the time she reached the child some minutes later, he was was well gone. As she stood there by the canal wondering what to think, Parent B came up and asked whether she had seen David, he must have wandered off.

Parent B's neighbour thus knows what happened that day by the canal; or at least she suspects what happened. But when she is interviewed by the police she fails to tell them of her suspicions. She convinces herself that she must have been mistaken. After all, Parent B is a good woman, she could not possibly have intended harm to her child.

Perhaps sometimes those who see evidence before their eyes that sexual abuse is taking place are rather like Parent B's neighbour. They see, they do not believe (they cannot believe), they re-interpret, they decide they are mistaken because otherwise how could they go on being friends with, being married to, loving, or working with, the person that they believe is abusing? You may wish to think again about the question of whether you would find it easy to report barely formed suspicions about a colleague or friend about which you had little evidence and which were so awful that you could barely contemplate them.

Another possible reason that caring staff might have for failing to act in relation to a colleague they suspect of abusing users might be that they feel sympathy for him. Consider, for example, Harry Chalmers whose value in the large residential setting in which he worked as a gardener was recognised by everyone and extended well beyond his formal duties.

Although in many ways his attitude towards residents was considered to be quaintly overprotective, Harry was given more responsibility for their care than would be usual for a man in his position. He liked them and enjoyed teaching them to work in the garden; they loved him and trusted him without question. The support of his colleagues and the high regard in which they held him, along with the affection of his wide circle of special friends, had for years helped Harry to cope with the growing problems in his marriage. It also gave him the opportunity to spend time alone with many residents, including Lizzy who had worked in the garden with him for years and liked to take him his tea at break time. The combination of these two aspects of his life – a troubled and failing marriage in which physical intimacy had ceased to play a part, and close friendships with residents and the opportunity to spend time alone with them – eventually resulted in an incident between Harry and Lizzy in which an affectionate hug, offered one day when Lizzy went to Harry seeking comfort after a disappointment, turned into inappropriate touching.

Despite the fact that Harry had not only been accused of abuse but had admitted that he had done what Lizzy said he did, many colleagues felt some sympathy for him, and we are inclined to agree with their point of view. Perhaps you might care to consider how you feel about Harry and his situation. Would you have felt inclined to report him if it had been you that Lizzy had inadvertently told about this incident some weeks after it occurred? Or, knowing what we have shared about his nature and long standing commitment to the care of residents, and about the things that were happening in his private life, would you have felt more inclined to take some other kind of action – for example, to have a quiet word with him about how unwise he had been on this occasion, warning him against any further lapses?

Though no-one with whom we have discussed these events has felt inclined to believe that what Harry did was okay, many have expressed sympathy for him. However, they are less likely to be sympathetic towards the staff member in the following story:

Melanie had learning difficulties and had lived in a large institution for most of her life. She was ignorant of and about sex but, after persistent pestering by a member of staff in the small hostel in which she now lived, she gave in to his advances and allowed him to have sexual intercourse with her on a number of occasions.

Staff caring for people like Melanie should not take advantage of their position of power, authority and trust to have sex with them, and so it is unequivocally the case (in our opinion at any rate) that the staff member in question was guilty of abuse, not only of Melanie but of the position of trust in which he was placed. This is so even if, in the end, Melanie not only agreed to have sex with him but wanted to do so.

But perhaps we might be persuaded to feel sympathy towards a person whose situation shared some similarity with that of Melanie and the man who took advantage of her. Consider, for example, the following story in which a worker in a small hostel has sex with a female resident.

George is Sarah's key worker and has developed a special fondness for her. He is young and idealistic though inexperienced, and has been helping Sarah to prepare to leave the hostel in which she has been living and to set up her own flat nearby. Recently they have paid several visits to the flat together to prepare meals and get it ready for her to move in. One evening when George is on night duty alone Sarah makes advances to him and he succumbs.

In this situation, although we might condemn George's actions, it is difficult not to have some inclination to believe that he had been more stupid than wicked in allowing himself to be seduced. He was a young and inexperienced worker who cared about users and had idealistic beliefs about treating them as people in their own right, with hopes and dreams, abilities and aspirations. Unlike the man who abused Melanie, George did not plan what happened between him and Sarah but was caught unawares by her. It is always morally wrong for workers to have sex with clients.[5] But sometimes it is possible to have sympathy even for those who do wrong.

Before leaving George, it is also worth noting the culpability of the agency in which he worked, in relation to the incident between him and Sarah. At the time of the incident, George was not really experienced enough in the work he was carrying out to have been given the onerous responsibility of taking full charge on his own of the small hostel in which he worked and in which Sarah lived. This was especially true in view of the fact that the hostel was a mixed sex one, and there was always the possibility that incidents might occur in which male workers alone on the premises would have to deal with female residents in intimate situations at a time of day when back-up was not readily available. George's relative inexperience, combined with observation of the way in which Sarah related to him and other circumstances before this incident, might have given careful managers reason to think twice before leaving this young man in sole charge. Or, at any rate, it would have given them reason, had they reflected on such matters sufficiently, to have talked frankly enough with him to have alerted him to the risks to which he could be exposed when alone with the resident group overnight[6]. This could have been done without offence or reflection on his professionalism because there was no obvious reason for anyone to have been worried about George's character, merely about the fact that the situation in which he was being placed was one which would have demanded caution even from a very experienced staff member.

It is interesting to speculate about the way we might react if a situation similar to that in which George found himself occurred between an inexperienced female member of staff and a young man with learning difficulties who made advances to her. What if, rather than simply making advances, he took the initiative in a way that she found quite unacceptable? Or what if the inexperienced member of staff to whom Sarah had made advances and who allowed herself to be seduced had been a woman rather than a man? Does the gender of the people involved in such a situation make any difference to the way that we think about it? Should it?

It is worth digressing from our storytelling mode for a moment to draw attention to what we consider to be a challenging idea from Brown and Turk's paper 'Defining Sexual Abuse as it Affects Adults with Learning

Disabilities' (Brown and Turk, 1992). In this very interesting article the authors show themselves to be bold enough to tackle several highly contentious taboo and nearly taboo subjects, and we shall refer to it again presently when discussing the problems of definition in relation to sexual abuse. For the moment we want to focus on their discussion of sexual relationships between a person with learning difficulties and a member of staff in a residential setting because, though interesting and important, we consider it to be flawed.

First, we think that their analysis of whether such relationships might be considered proper conflates two important and problematic areas – one concerned with the propriety or otherwise of sexual relationships between people with learning difficulties and staff, the other with the propriety or otherwise of sex between people with learning difficulties and typical citizens.

Second, although Brown and Turk are obviously well intentioned in exploring the possibility of meaningful, consensual and non-abusive sexual relationships between people who have learning difficulties and those who do not, there are shortcomings in their analysis of power relations in service settings. They accept that a power imbalance between a member of professional staff and a resident in such a setting rules out the possibility of sexual behaviour between them, even where the resident seems to be 'willingly consenting'; yet they seem to be ready to make an exception in the case of staff whose status in the service setting, by virtue of being low paid or being unpaid, could be considered to be lower. There are dangers in making generalisations about who does and who does not wield power in service settings and about who can and who cannot have sex with people with learning difficulties, simply because their job either does or does not carry with it officially invested power. Power within organisations is not like that, and in organisations dealing with people this is especially true.

There is a joke within educational circles that, whatever the governors of a school think, the caretaker is really the person who runs it; and we are aware of situations where, despite the presence of highly educated, trained and paid psychiatrists, psychologists, nurses and other professionals, the person who wields most power over day to day events in some hospital and other residential care settings is an unqualified auxiliary nurse, or member of care staff, or cleaner, or cook. Voluntary workers and other workers of low given status, just as much as those in a hierarchically elevated position, can wield power over a person with learning difficulties, and as a result they could abuse them by having sex with them.

Consider, for example, the staff member who raped Allison. He was not a professional; his role as a driver was not one of high status or standing.

All he was paid to do was to collect and deliver users safely. And yet he wielded power over Allison in the most overt and brutal way. Of course, we are not being entirely fair here because this man clearly raped Allison, and Brown and Turk are certainly not condoning rape.

In other stories that we have told where a staff member has had sexual contact with a service user, we have indicated that there are some circumstances which might lead us to deal less harshly with the offender. For example, we feel some sympathy for Harry Chalmers, whose career as a respected and respectable gardener was ruined as a result of one mistake with a woman for whom he had cared deeply over a long period, and who thought nothing of the change to the way in which he embraced her that day when she went to him upset and worried. But we do not feel sorry for Harry because we condone what he did or on the basis that he was of low given status but because what he did lacked a feature that seems to us to be important in determining the nature of acts as abusive – that it did not involve a readiness to take advantage of the person with whom he had sexual contact.

Although we have sympathy for Harry, we believe that he should not have done what he did. It is not that we believe that he had bad intentions towards Lizzy. Indeed, if Harry had reached retirement age (which he did a few months after he was sacked as the result of this unfortunate incident) and had then begun courting Lizzy, we would have had no qualms about their blossoming relationship. However, at the time that the incident occurred, he had a relationship to Lizzy that precluded the possibility of sexual contact, even of the mildest kind, taking place between them; that is why we think he was wrong if not wicked.

Brown and Turk obviously share some of our concerns. They believe that staff should be given clear guidance about the fact that relationships between service users and staff should be precluded until such time as services are able to 'engage competently' in open discussion (p49) about the power balance in any developing sexual relationships. For our part, even if such open discussion could be achieved, we are sceptical whether any case could be made for permitting sexual relationships between staff and residents. The only safe way of thinking about sex between people with learning difficulties and those who are charged with helping to provide care for them whether by formal employment or because they have volunteered, is to think that it should not occur, and that if it does it should be considered wrong and possibly abusive.

Abuse in a day care setting

Peter Green abused the men in his care although he did not lay hands on them. Against the conclusion that his actions were abusive, an apologist for Green might argue that what he did was relatively innocent because no-one was harmed either directly or indirectly. Her argument might continue that since Green merely watched people doing what they would have been doing anyway – showering and getting dressed and undressed – he did nothing wrong. We reject this conclusion because it was not necessary for him to watch the men in the way that he did, or at least it was not necessary in all instances.

Green's duties included overseeing users dressing and undressing in situations where they required physical assistance or where they were being helped to improve their personal hygiene. For some of the day centre users it was essential for him to carry out these duties by being in the room with them, but for others they could best be achieved by hovering attentively outside in the corridor, or by watching unobtrusively, perhaps via a mirror. It is because of these facts about the necessity for supervision in caring for at least some people with learning difficulties that Green's apologist would argue that he did no more than was necessary to ensure the safety and well being of the men in his care. But this is simply not true, because Green did more than that; rather than using the mirrors to enable him to make necessary observations of those men who required detailed supervision for reasons of safety, he used them to watch all the men. And what is more, he did it in order to feed his voyeuristic appetite.

Thus what makes Green's behaviour abusive is not the fact that he watched men at these times but his motivation in doing so. In other words, his actions must be deemed abusive because, however unobtrusively, he used the men with whom he worked and for whom he had the responsibility to care, in order to satisfy his own desires.

Green did not touch the men that he abused; but he abused them nevertheless. It is worth noting that, although the most obvious paradigm examples of sexual abuse involve contact, a member of staff working in a similar situation to Green could touch the men in his care in parts of the body that are considered private without creating any concerns about abuse having taken place. Where users require help with intimate physical care, touch is a necessary part of giving such help. It might even be the case that innocent touch that was part of routine care in dressing, bathing and drying could have erotic effects on the person being touched and still raise no questions of abuse. The fact that physical contact resulted in sexual arousal would not in itself mean that the contact was abusive. For certain people the paucity of stimulation in their life is such that some aspects of daily living – such as eating and bathing, taken for granted as routine by the rest of us – might for them be the sensual highlight of their lives. For it to be the case that contact producing sexual arousal in users should be considered as constituting sexual abuse, it would have to be performed at least partly with the intention of producing arousal. In addition, it would have to be performed because the person doing the touching gained sexual satisfaction in doing so, since there are situations in which it would be appropriate for professionals to touch with the intention of producing arousal; one of these would be where the touching took place as part of a plan of action aimed at assisting a person with severe learning disabilities to learn to masturbate properly.

Finally, Green's apologist might want to claim that, even if what he did was perverse and that he took advantage of the men in his care to satisfy his own desires, at least he did not harm them, because the men knew nothing about what he was doing. Thus she might claim that really he did nothing terribly wrong. Again we reject this. Even if no-one ever discovered what he was up to, even if the men in his care remained unaware of the way in which they were being used, even if Green's salacious interest never led to overt sexual abuse whether of a contact or non-contact kind, he acted badly simply because he used them as a means to his own sexual satisfaction. He treated them as objects to be used rather than as people to be related to, and that is unacceptable.

Whether or not they were aware or would ever have become aware of his actions, the men that Green abused were abused while they were attending a day centre. Allison was also abused by a member of staff, but there are differences between her situation and that of the men that Green abused. For one thing, whereas the men Green abused were not subjected to physical abuse and knew nothing of what was going on, Allison was physically assaulted, and it is unequivocally the case that she suffered as the result of her abuse. For another, she was abused away from the premises, by someone charged with responsibility for seeing her safely home after an evening out. It is these features of her story that mean that even though they agreed with our analysis of Green's actions as amounting to serious abuse, some people might be inclined to believe that the abuse perpetrated against Allison is more serious, more significant, more abusive, more wicked, because not only was she abused but she suffered as a result of abuse that was not only physical but violent.

Allison's story is a real one. A man whose responsibility it was to transport her from one place to another really did force sex on her. She was raped and this is plainly both morally and legally wrong, and, as a result of this incident, the driver lost his job and faced prosecution. Despite its obvious wrongness, one not uncommon reaction in relation to an incident of this kind is to ask whether the staff member in question – in this case the driver – had been adequately vetted before being put in charge of vulnerable people. This diverts attention from the individual who has committed the crime and suggests that, if an adequate procedure for vetting prospective staff is in place and is properly and meticulously carried out, potential perpetrators of such offences will not be employed. It also suggests that the driver who raped Allison might not have been adequately vetted and that therefore the department which employed him must be guilty of neglect in allowing him to have access to people like her. To pursue such a line of thought implies that an employer who fails to foresee the possibility that a prospective employee might perpetrate sexual offences against users is somehow just as guilty, and perhaps even more guilty, than the individual who perpetrated the offence. Such a line of reasoning is flawed. To our our mind an employer who failed, as the result of negligence, to screen out a prospective employee who had a criminal record, would be culpable if the employee then acted immorally or criminally. However, it is simply mistaken to believe that employers are necessarily in the wrong if they employ such a person.

When, as a result of unexpected events or human wickedness, harm comes to people who who are receiving care, questions are commonly asked about the part that negligence on the part of services might have played in allowing or even bringing about the situation. Criticising the caring professions in such circumstances has become a bloodsport for the media. Of course, agencies and institutions may be guilty of negligence in the way in which they have discharged their duty to care. However, diverting attention away from the sins of those who commit offences is unjust and unwise and most often unhelpful. While critical analysis of the procedures and guidelines that govern the behaviour of professional carers and the extent to which they have acted diligently in performing their tasks is necessary at times, making this the central focus after incidents of the kind we are discussing can deflect attention away from those who have acted badly.

One area in which this bloodsport is engaged in particularly frequently is child care. Where children have been violently abused within families there is a tendency to scrutinise not only social work procedures but also social work practice. In such cases it seems to be the rule that social workers always do what is wrong. If they take children away from parents because there are grounds for suspecting abuse, they are likely to be criticised for heavy handed interference. On the other hand, in situations where children left with their parents and carers are abused, social workers are likely to be villified for failing to take action even when there were only the slimmest grounds for suspecting the possibility of abuse.

While it is undoubtedly important to ensure that social workers and the agencies for which they work have done the best they can, focusing attention on the possibility that they have been negligent or have made mistakes, or on the possibility that procedures are inadequate, has the effect of diverting attention away from the fact that some parents do at times act badly towards their children. An additional consequence of this tendency is that neighbours and others who have contact with the family might fail to maintain the sense of community responsibility that is necessary if we are to have a society in which human frailty and wickedness are adequately addressed.

That it is not just the media that maintain odd ideas about the allocation of reponsibility in relation to such stories may be seen by considering the conclusions of an article in the *Journal of Applied Philosophy* in which Hollis and Howe (1987) have argued that in child care cases in which parents do great harm to children, social workers who had responsibility for these children are necessarily responsible for the harm that they suffer, whether or not they fulfilled their responsibilities to the best of their ability and according to guidelines provided for such work. They write:

> the final question is whether the social worker is morally at fault for her decisions, when they turn out badly because the system licences greater risks than welfare alone would approve. Our harsh verdict is Yes. She became a social worker by her own choice and, even if her predicament dawned on her only in midstream, she chose to continue. She has accepted the constraints and is making judgements which would reconcile the conflicts, only if they displayed a professional accuracy which, in the present state of knowledge, they cannot possess. Because there is such a thing as pure luck, like being struck by lightning, there is usually a corresponding doubt whether bad consequences are the fault of bad judgement. But the doubt does not cover all the cases and she knows that sometimes she has intervened and done harm. The failures are not hers alone but hers they remain. (p132)

Let us return to Allison's story. Presumably Hollis and Howe and any who share their view would argue that, because of the uncertainty that is inherent in vetting candidates for posts that involve caring for people with learning difficulties, authorities and departments and institutions – and individual managers – are *responsible* for the harm that comes to users as the result of sexual abuse perpetrated by staff. Presumably they would argue that those who should or could have vetted Alison's rapist when he applied for employment are responsible for what he did to her because they failed to spot his potential for abuse, and consequently failed to refuse him employment on the grounds that they could see, whether by looking into a crystal ball or by some other means, that he was that kind of man; and what is more they took on the job of their own free will and even if their predicament (the difficulties of being sure who will and who won't turn out to be an abuser) 'dawned on them only in midstream', they 'chose to continue'.

No procedure for vetting staff can be foolproof to the extent that it can prevent someone who is both intent on furthering his own wicked ends and clever enough to deceive others about his motivation and intentions. Not only that, but it is entirely possible that a person who at the time of vetting was innocent of any evil intent could, at a later date, opportunistically begin to engage in unacceptable and abusive behaviour when the occasion presented itself. It is also possible that, as the result of ongoing aspects of his home life, a person might change in ways that led to his beginning to prey on those in his charge. Indeed something of this kind was true in relation to Allison's rapist, whose life and relationships were in such chaos that when the chance arose he turned his attentions to Allison, who was easy prey.

Whatever the truth of the matter: whether the authority was guilty of neglect because they failed to spot him as a potential rapist, and whether he planned to rape Allison or simply took the opportunity when it arose in a spur of the moment kind of way, the driver abused both Allison and the trust that had been placed in him. In spite of this, it is interesting to note that, although in the mind of the service manager there was no question that the driver had committed a grave offence, some staff at the social education centre thought that he had been somewhat harshly handled, not only because he was successfully prosecuted for rape but even because he had lost his job over the incident. It is interesting to speculate about the reasons why this should have been so. One reason was perhaps that the driver was a popular man who was so warm and generous with the users that his colleagues may have found it difficult to believe that he could have forced himself on Allison. Another might be that they could not get rid of the feeling that perhaps the driver had just taken the regular friendly interactions that had gone on between him and Allison over the years a bit too far. They may even have felt guilty about their part in encouraging the friendship that had developed between the driver and Allison – by referring to him as her 'boyfriend' in the kind of innocent and cheerful (though perhaps tasteless and unwise) banter that is not uncommon. It is interesting also to ask the question whether these same staff would have been so willing to forgive the driver if the person he had raped (or with whom he 'had sex', because that was the way they talked about it rather than 'rape'; 'rape' is such a distasteful and upsetting word, isn't it?) had been a person without a learning disability – perhaps even one of them – rather than one of the people that he was paid to transport to and fro. Or what if, rather than being Allison's parents' daughter, the person raped had been *their* daughter? Our guess is that in any of these scenarios, forgiveness, even understanding, would have been more difficult to reach.

Abuse of people with learning difficulties living with support in the community

Since the 1950s there has been a move away from care in institutions to care in the community, predominantly because of a growing critique of institutional life. Along with this there has been a growth in the belief that people who had previously been marginalised should be afforded the opportunities of ordinary life; this belief and the values that underpin it are perhaps most vigorously and coherently expressed in the work of the proponents of normalisation and of its more recent successor social role valorisation. Giving people with learning difficulties the opportunity to live in ordinary domestic situations clearly offers the possibility of positive benefits. It provides a jumping off point for all the advantages of ordinary life, including friendships, employment and leisure opportunities. But community care can put its beneficiaries at risk of exploitation and abuse in a different way, but with the same brutal consequences as the old institutions, and this raises important questions for the managers of the new style services.

The staff of supported accommodation, and the agencies which provide and inspect it, have a dual responsibility both to foster independence and to protect from harm. It is for this reason that it could be argued that, just as much as David, people like Lillian and Charles are doubly abused; that they are abused not only by those who take sexual advantage of them but also by a system which, by failing to take sufficient account of the risks to which they are exposed and by putting them into inadequately monitored living situations, perhaps actually exposes them to risk. There are various ways in which the community care system can do this. Consider first what happened to Lillian, who was living in a supported flat but had a large degree of freedom and responsibility for deciding what she did, when, and with whom.

Lillian had a significant intellectual disability. This fact, and the fact that she did not understand the imbalance in power between her and the men with whom she was engaging in sex, suggests that, whatever she thought was going on, the men were abusing her by using her as the means to their own sexual gratification. It seems likely that they thought that because she was 'a bit simple' she would be 'an easy lay'. Given this interpretation of Lillian's story it is clear that the men who had sex with her are to be morally disapproved of. They took advantage of a woman with learning difficulties; perhaps they also took advantage of the fact that though she had some basic social skills she was clearly looking for affection.

But is this necessarily the true interpretation of what went on between

Lillian and her 'friends'? In coming to the conclusion that they abused her and that she was abused by them, we have made assumptions about the motives and intentions of these men and also about Lillian's understanding of the situation. But perhaps these assumptions are unreasonable. What if these men thought of Lillian simply as a woman who was keen for a bit of male company and enjoyed having sex with more than one man at once? In that case, though we might find their behaviour distasteful and even disapprove of it morally – on the grounds, for example, that we believe that sex between people is proper only when there are two players and no more, it might seem harsh to accuse these men of having abused Lillian. To someone familiar with people with learning difficulties and aware of her intellectual level, it might seem obvious that Lillian was incapable of understanding the nature of her relationship with these men. However, if they believed that she was just a woman who liked a bit of fun, then having sex with her either on a regular basis, or even for a 'one night stand', however offensive to those of us who do not share their idea of what is proper in the area of sexual morality, might for them have seemed relatively ordinary. And however morally offensive to most people, their actions could not be morally disapproved of on the basis that they were taking advantage of her intellectual disability.

It may be a bit difficult to get to grips with the idea that a person with learning difficulties who is picked up in a bar and ends up having sex with a group of men, might not be the subject of sexual abuse. But suppose instead that Lillian had developed her 'nodding acquaintanceship' in the bar not with a group of men but with only one man. She gets to know him and in due course he invites her back to his flat where she has sex with him willingly, even enthusiastically. How are we to decide whether this constitutes abuse? Lillian is the same person, her characteristics and experience are the same, but the social taboo or feeling of discomfort or disapproval commonly associated with the idea of group sex, which was present in the original scenario, is absent in this new situation in which only one man has become involved with her. The deciding factors here are more likely to be concerned with the characteristics of the man – his motives and intentions, his perceptions of Lillian and how he understands the relationship between them, and the events that have occurred. Perhaps there is a continuum between abuse and innocent sexual involvement in such a situation.

Firstly, if this man engaged in conversation with Lillian because, like the men in the original scenario, he realised that she had a learning disability and believed that this would make her easy to seduce, then he would undoubtedly be guilty of abuse no matter how sweetly he wooed her; and this would be the case even if Lillian was a willing partner in the sexual encounter, even if she had made as much effort to seduce him as he made to seduce her. If, on the other hand, the man engaged Lillian in conversation, realised that she had learning difficulties but nonetheless found her attractive and enjoyed her company, to think of their encounter as abusive would be inappropriate. Indeed, provided Lillian felt the same way about him, if their friendship developed into a sexual relationship whether immediately or at some time in the future, it seems to us that, given the views we express about the possibility of sex between people with learning difficulties and ordinary people in Part Four, we would feel compelled to consider their relationship positively (though what right we might have to express any opinion on the sex lives of two private citizens is of course questionable).

There are a number of other possibilities. If the man found Lillian attractive and believed honestly that he could care for her, or even simply lusted after her but failed to reflect on her intellectual state, then whatever our own views of the morality of casual sexual encounters, to consider his actions in seducing her as abuse would seem unwarranted. If, however, he found Lillian attractive and liked her so much that he was glad that she seemed 'a bit slow', because that allowed him to seduce her more easily, not only into having sex but hopefully into an ongoing relationship, then, in spite of the fact that at one level his intentions towards her were honourable because he hoped that their relationship might continue, his actions in having sex with her would be abusive. On the other hand, given the fact that he cared for Lillian and hoped to form a longer term relationship with her, we might have some inclination to consider him as being naughty rather than nasty, as a rascal rather than as a rogue.

In all of the variations of Lillian's story that we have discussed, two features have remained constant. In each case we have made the assumption that the people with whom she had sexual encounters were men without learning difficulties – regular, ordinary men, who 'picked her up' in a bar. It is worth, finally, contemplating whether it would make any difference to the way in which we would judge what went on between Lillian and her various companions if they had been people with learning difficulties, and also whether it would make any difference if the people with whom she became involved had been women rather than men. We leave this for you to ponder but with two observations. First, we think that it should make no difference if the men had learning difficulties; what would make a difference would be the way in which they understood their encounter with Lillian and the extent to which their actions were manipulative of her as an object to be used, or affirmative of her as a person to be related to. Second, in relation to the possibility that Lillian's sexual encounters with friends from the pub should have been lesbian rather than heterosexual in nature, we think the same rules must apply in coming to decisions about whether the sex that took place was abusive or not, despite the fact that had her lover or lovers been female, no possibility of prosecution would have been present for them.

If Lillian was sexually abused, she was abused because the men with whom she had sex took advantage of her intellectual level to persuade her (to seduce her?) into having sex with them. If she was abused she was abused because they pretended to be her friends in order to get what they wanted. Charles was also abused by people who either were or pretended to be his friends. However, as with Peter Green, the staff member in a day centre who systematically abused the men in his care by re-arranging mirrors to allow him to watch them dressing and bathing, Charles's neighbours were involved in sexual abuse of a non-contact kind. They did not touch Charles or expect or encourage him to touch them; nevertheless they used him as a means to their own sexual satisfaction and hence were abusers. If they had been challenged about what they thought they were up to, they would probably have pointed out that Charles enjoyed watching these movies like any normal hot blooded young man. This may well have been true. But even if it was, it does not excuse their behaviour in inviting him to watch these movies with them, which was aimed not at giving Charles a good time but at giving themselves a good time by watching him having a good time.

It is entirely possible that the sessions in which Charles engaged with his neighbours started relatively innocently. It might be the case that in the first instance the neighbours sought his involvement as 'one of the boys'. They may well have befriended him innocently, perhaps even without realising that he had a learning disability. Though many of us would consider it perverse to enjoy watching pornographic movies with one's friends, Charles's neighbours may have been in the habit of doing so and for them there would thus have been nothing unusual and certainly nothing immoral about it. If this was the case and they were unaware that Charles had learning difficulties then there may well have been nothing abusive about their behaviour. However, if after a while they eventually concluded that Charles was 'a bit simple' but continued with their sessions because they gained sexual satisfaction by watching his arousal then this would be sexually abusive behaviour.

It is important to note that the offence of which we think the neighbours are guilty is not that of encouraging Charles to watch risqué movies; it is that of using Charles as a means to producing sexual satisfaction for themselves. It is also important to note that even if the satisfaction that Charles's neighbours gained was not sexual in nature – if, say, they had simply enjoyed having a laugh at the way in which he got himself all excited and perhaps embarrassed when watching the movies with them, we think that they would have been guilty of abuse. Not only that, but the abuse of which they would have been guilty, even in such a scenario, would have been sexual abuse – because gaining the pleasure they did involved misusing him sexually.

Finally it is worth noting the possible involvement of community support workers in situations such as that of Charles and his neighbours. With the best of intentions support workers might, by the very process of working hard at enabling friendships to develop between clients with learning difficulties and residents in the locality, actually bring about situations in which people with learning difficulties are abused. Given the credence and weight that is given to facilitating real friendships between people with learning difficulties living independently and regular people, it is possible that workers might be so pleased at seeing relationships developing between users and local people that they could give every encouragement for them to continue while failing adequately to monitor them. It might even be the case that they would believe, on ideological grounds, that it is really none of their business who service users befriend and are befriended by, and that to try to dictate who they befriend and what they do with them, involves the unreasonable imposition of middle class professional values.

Care in the community has undoubtedly brought many real benefits to people like Lillian and Charles, who in an earlier time would in all probability have lived out their lives in segregation from their ordinary peers. It is because of this that many community care staff are ideologically committed to the belief that services that allow users to live lives that are as ordinary as possible, in contexts that are as ordinary as possible, are superior to services that echo the large scale residential care of yesterday. And it is because of their ideological commitments that they may find it difficult to acknowledge that living in non-sheltered and non-protective community settings carries risks as well as benefits. The stories about Charles and Lillian illustrate some of the risks that people like them may face when they are befriended by ordinary people such as neighbours or casual acquaintances in however limited a way. But the sexual dangers encountered by some people with learning difficulties living in the community may be much more direct and even violent, as was the case with Stella, a young woman who was returning to the Housing Association flat that she shared with two other women with learning difficulties after an evening at the local speedway racing track.

As Stella was leaving the speedway track, a man she had never met before followed her and told her that he would see her safely home. Stella accepted his offer because, ironically as it turned out, she was aware of the dangers of walking home alone and wanted to avoid the possibility of being accosted by some unsavoury character. Her escort did not see her home safely; nor did he invite her to come into the park with him or to have sex with him. Rather he dragged her into the park, beat her up and raped her.

The situation in which Stella was raped is an example of the stereotypical 'stranger danger' scenario about which children and other vulnerable people must be warned and in relation to which they must be educated. She put her trust in someone she had perhaps noticed casually during the evening at the track and possibly considered as being part of the same crowd, although she had not spoken with him before. He took advantage of her gullible nature to get himself into a position where he could abuse her.

The possibility of abuse of this kind is frightening and many professional staff fear that to acknowledge the kind of explicit sexual dangers experienced by Stella and others like her would be to invite those elements of the media and general public who are opposed to the policy of community care to call for its reversal on the grounds of danger to the individual men and women concerned. Any move that resulted in the re-emergence of institutional patterns of care, or that slowed down the development of dispersed supported accommodation, would go against their ideological grain. But more importantly they would suggest, and we would agree, that such regresssive moves would serve the interests of users less well. Though it is not our intention to act as apologists for governments, it is important to note that even in a situation where levels of support in the community were as favourable as any that we could wish for, it would not be possible wholly to control and to monitor the risks to which people in community living situations are exposed. Rather than ignoring the problems for fear of the consequences of being open about them, we thus believe that it is necessary for those who work in community care explicitly to address the kinds of dangers exemplified by the stories of Charles and Lillian and Stella, and if necessary to do so in the public arena.

Abusers and perpetrators: one and the same?

In illustrating some of the ethical issues that the sexual abuse of people with learning difficulties raises, we have shared and discussed stories about sexual abuse of different kinds, drawn from a number of different contexts. In doing so we have tried to reflect the complexity of these issues and also the complexity of questions relating to the definition of sexual abuse which we shall address again later. We want now to discuss the possibility that there could be sexual abuse without an abuser, and also the possibility that there could be an abuser without abuse being experienced. Let us consider these possibilities in turn.

Abuse without an abuser

It is at least imaginable that there might be situations in which abuse takes place without there being any abuser; in other words there could be times when a person experiences abuse but where the person who brings about that experience does not abuse. One situation in which it could make sense to think like this would be one in which a person with learning difficulties uses another person sexually, but with no real notion that what he is doing is wrong, or even that the person towards whom he acts in this way objects or may be terrified by what he is doing. Such a person could realistically be considered to be a perpetrator of sexual abuse because the other person experiences his actions as abusive. On the other hand, although he has perpetrated abuse, his poor understanding of what he has done and its significance for the other person means that he is innocent of wrongdoing even though he has caused the other harm. And thus it seems unjust and inaccurate to describe him as an abuser because he has not abused, although his actions have.

Consider, for example, the following story in which a series of encounters between two boys in a residential school for pupils with learning difficulties become unbearable for one.

> Hugh was ten years old and Gerry was fourteen but despite the age gap between them their friendship had been encouraged by the staff in their residential school. It blossomed further when they were given the opportunity to share a bedroom. Though they began to spend most of their time together away from the other children, the staff had no reason to suspect that there was anything untoward about this because it was perfectly ordinary for older and younger children to form close relationships with one another. And so it came as a bit of a shock to them when Hugh arrived in class after break one day looking flushed and tearful, crying and saying that Gerry wasn't his friend any more. After some encouragement he told staff that Gerry had been bullying him. Then he said, 'Gerry keeps making me do things with his willie and he keeps touching mine and it's sore and he's not my friend any more.'

It is clear that Gerry had forced Hugh into sexual activities in which he did not want to engage. As a result Hugh was deeply unhappy. In a situation like this the staff clearly had to intervene because, whatever the true description of the way Gerry was acting towards Hugh, it was making Hugh miserable and that had to be stopped. The question of whether Gerry was a sexual abuser is more difficult to deal with. Whatever the legalities of the situation, the answer to this question depends on the level of understanding that both he and Hugh had of the nature of their relationship, and their respective understandings about what was going on between them. It is clear that Hugh was sexually abused because, whether or not he understood the nature of the behaviours in which Gerry was forcing him to engage, he didn't want to engage in them. However, it is perhaps less clear that Gerry was a sexual abuser because his developmental immaturity calls into question whether he understood what he was doing sufficiently to be considered as a person who had acted abusively. In order to decide that he was an abuser, we would want to be sure both that he understood that the consent of the other person is a prerequisite for intimate behaviour and that he realised that Hugh did not want to engage with him in this way.

Another example of a situation in which it might make sense to think that what has occurred has been abuse without an abuser is that of David, whose story was discussed earlier. You will recall that David was raped over a long period while living in a mental handicap hospital. Although there is no doubt that his assailants took advantage of his inability to resist being used for their gratification, we might ask whether they were necessarily abusers. After all, they were themselves men with learning disabilities and so the question arises whether they had sufficient understanding of what they were doing and the effect it was having on David to be thought of as abusers. If they failed to comprehend the significance of their actions or, for example, misconstrued David's compliance as a routine act carried out as a trade for sweets or cigarettes, or were unable to interpret verbal or non-verbal signs from David that he objected to or wished them to stop doing what they were doing, then we might decide that this was an example of abuse being experienced by a person but where the perpetrators should not be described as abusers.

What we have said about the possibility that a person with learning difficulties could be a perpetrator of sexual abuse without being an abuser should not be taken as an indication that we believe that, as a general rule, people with learning difficulties cannot sexually abuse others. If we were to think that people with learning difficulties who engage in such behaviour can never be deemed to be abusers then where would we stand in relation to the proposition that people with learning difficulties should be treated in the same way as other citizens in respect of their sexuality? The conditions that would determine whether a regular person is a sexual abuser will also count in the case of a person with learning difficulties.

It is relatively easy to to come to terms with the idea that it is inappropriate to think of someone who cannot understand the nature of his actions or the social rules that govern sexual behaviour as an abuser, when he acts towards another in a way that is experienced as abusive, when the very same actions would justify this conclusion were they performed by a person who did have the necessary understanding. It is perhaps more difficult to get to grips with the idea that an ordinary person who did have the necessary level of understanding could also perpetrate sexual abuse that is suffered by another but without being an abuser. However, this might be the case. Consider, for example, someone who acted with regard for another person as a person in an encounter that they took to be mutually focused on sexual fulfilment while the other person had failed to understand the extent and nature of his companion's interest in him. Imagine that taking the initiative one evening the first person began making sexual advances. Imagine further, that the second person, realising what was going on too late – to put a stop to things, found himself engaging in a sexual act that he found repugnant – not because he did not care for or have regard for his companion, but because the nature of his care and his agenda for their relationship would not have led him to engage in sex. The fact that he failed to make clear that he did not want to engage in the sexual act in question would not in itself make the other an abuser, even if, throughout the act, he was experiencing revulsion and feeling abused.[7]

An abuser but no victim

There is more than one type of situation in which there could be an abuser without anyone being abused. Consider again the story of Peter Green, who manipulated the people in his care in order to satisfy his voyeuristic tastes and who was guilty of abuse in spite of the fact that the people he abused knew nothing of what was going on. This is one of a number of situations in which although abuse is carried out, it is carried out without awareness on the part of the subject so that, although an abuser acts in ways that constitute abuse, his actions are not experienced as abusive.

Another kind of situation where it might be argued that there could be an abuser without a victim or victims of abuse would be where a person takes advantage of another in order to satisfy his sexual appetites but where that other enjoys what goes on between them. Consider, for example, David's story to which we have already referred. What if David had enjoyed the contact he had with the men who raped him[8], rather than finding it abhorrent? Could the fact that those who raped him had given him pleasure make us inclined to think that he was not a victim of sexual abuse?

The use and abuse of David, by others, might be rationalised as having been of benefit to him because it gave him contact and physical stimulation that was otherwise missing from his life. There is some similarity between this idea and some ways in which it is possible to view the rape of a young woman in a catatonic state, portrayed in Dennis Potter's television play *Brimstone and Treacle,* which was scheduled for screening by the BBC in 1976 but did not appear until August 1987. In the play the young woman whose condition, it was believed, had been brought about as the result of a road accident in which she was knocked down by a car, is regularly abused by a young man who wheedles his way into her home by persuading her parents that he is a friend from her student days. As audience, we are faced with a dilemma of conscience because the sexual assaults to which the young rogue subjects this woman eventually force her out of the catatonic state – which we then learn came about as the result of shock at discovering her father having sex at his workplace. As audience we are challenged to consider whether the wicked act of rape against this defenceless person can be retrospectively justified by the fact that it awakens her from her slumber.

Although the acts of the villain in Potter's play appeared to have good side effects, we do not believe this means that he may be excused; his intention was abusive and wicked and his acts infringed in the most awful way on his victim. Nor do we think that in the case where their understanding is sufficient to warrant thinking of them as abusers the men who raped David could be excused, even if he had enjoyed the physical stimulation he gained from their attention. In neither of these stories does the fact or possibility of imposed sex having good effects take away the guilt of those who perpetrated it; nor does it make their actions less abusive, or make them any less abusers. Good outcomes that follow from bad deeds do not change the moral nature of those deeds, nor the moral character of those who enact them. A murderer, who by shooting his target saves him the bother of ending his miserable life by suicide, which he intended to do that night with the pills he had just bought from the chemist, might do his victim a favour but this neither takes away his guilt as a murderer nor makes his act a good one. And a person who forces sex on another, or otherwise engages in sexually abusive behaviour towards him, is a sexual abuser just because he does so; the fact that his despicable behaviour might have good repercussions does not mean that he acts rightly or even that he should be excused.

Unpalatable as it might be to think about, if sufficient evidence became available supporting the contention that some forms of enforced sexual activity had a therapeutic effect, this might lead to the suggestion that the possibility of some kind of sex therapy which involved physical contact was worthwhile investigating. Such therapy might then become part of the battery of techniques available to physiotherapists or psychotherapists or nurses. The question of what form such therapy might take, who might be expected to undertake it, and how it could be developed, investigated and put into practice in a way that was ethically acceptable, poses problems that it is beyond the scope of this book to consider. We find this idea so morally offensive that we thought hard before including it in this book. We think that our moral offence at the idea is probably longlasting, based as it is on other ideas about the propriety of enforcing treatment on people that they do not wish to receive. However, it is possible that some people who have worked within the legislation relating to the treatment of psychiatric patients on an involuntary basis might see ways round this if they were convinced that treatment of this kind could be justified and ethically carried out.

What is 'sexual abuse'?

In discussing the stories about people to whom we have introduced you, we have been trying both to map out the territory that is covered by the term 'sexual abuse' and to raise some of the ethical issues with which this most distressing of human phenomena presents us as professional carers, as relatives of people with learning difficulties, and as citizens who share communal responsibility if not for the evils of our society then for what is done to combat them. We want now to say something about the problems of definition because, in itself, the question of whether an adequate definition of sexual abuse can be constructed is one with ethical consequences.

Brown and Turk (1992) assert that 'In order for professionals to develop a coherent response to sexual abuse in services for people with learning difficulties, there must first be a debate about what we are calling 'abuse'.' (p44) We agree. If it cannot be said simply and clearly what is to count as sexual abuse, then it will obviously be more difficult both to pinpoint instances and to deal in appropriate ways with abusers; and, perhaps even more importantly, unless we are clear what constitutes abuse, we will be less able to help and care for those who have been victims of sexual abuse. Unfortunately, the issue of what constitutes sexual abuse is a good deal more complex than many people seem to think. And so, although we think that it would be a good thing if a simple definition could be given of sexual abuse in the same way that a definition can be given of acts such as swimming, sky diving and suicide (see Fairbairn, 1995), it is doubtful whether a wholly successful definition is possible. It is not that we do not know what sexual abuse is; indeed, like many other people we are fairly sure that we could say of most acts whether they constitute sexual abuse or not. Nevertheless, saying that we have a good idea what constitutes abuse is not the same as saying that we can draw up a template against which others can measure acts that may be abusive in a way that will allow them successfully to partition off abusive from non-abusive acts.

The terminology of abusive acts

We believe that the terminology used in relation to the kinds of actions that might be termed sexually abusive should be the same no matter what the age or intellectual ability of the person who is thought to have been abused. Given this, it is interesting to note the title of Brown and Turk's article about the definition of abuse: 'Defining sexual abuse as it affects adults with learning difficulties' (Brown and Turk, 1992). This seems to imply that sexual abuse might be defined differently depending on the group on which attention is focused. This is curious. Imagine what we would think about someone who purported to offer a definition of 'theft as it affects people who are well off' (as opposed to 'theft as it affects people who are poor'). More seriously, and more pertinently, consider what women living in violent marriages (or other women) would think of an article which purported to define 'rape as it affects women within marriage'. Of course, Brown and Turk may be trying to take account of the fact that in relation to adults without learning disabilities certain kinds of sexual abuse would normally be referred to more simply – as, for example, 'rape' or 'indecent assault', and of the fact that certain kinds of actions that in relation to typical citizens would not be considered abusive at all might be abusive if their subject had learning disabilities. They are probably, also, being mindful of the fact that concern with sexual abuse, until relatively recently, has been mainly focused on the sexual abuse of children. But rape is rape and sexual abuse is sexual abuse no matter whether the person has learning difficulties, is an adult or a child.

Abuse that involves assault and abuse that does not

It seems important to raise questions about the way in which sexual assaults and the sexual misuse of people are labelled, because whereas 'assault' and following years of consciousness raising by women 'rape' carry with them a strong association with violence and of serious damage being done to one person by another, 'abuse' somehow suggests something less violent, less harmful, less serious. We would argue that many instances of sexual abuse should be referred to as 'sexual assault' or 'rape', which they are. But we do not want to see the expression 'sexual abuse' disappear. Rather we want to argue for a wider use of this term. For the moment, however, we want to say something about those instances of sexual abuse that involve assault and could equally be referred to, therefore, as 'rape' or 'sexual assault' depending on the particular circumstances.

Why should sexual assaults of different kinds be labelled in different ways? For example, why should it be the case that when adults who do not have learning difficulties are sexually assaulted we talk plainly in terms of 'sexual assault' or 'rape', whereas when children or adults with learning difficulties are sexually assaulted we are more likely to refer to it as 'sexual abuse? And why, in relation to the most recent species of sexual assault that has been admitted or discovered to be a problem – that perpetrated against elderly people, should we again talk of abuse rather than plain assault or rape? Of course, there are well publicised cases of rape in which the victims are elderly though interestingly these are usually cases where the attack has been carried out by an unknown intruder into the elderly person's home. In marked contrast to this, rape involving an elderly person when it occurs within the family, or in a care setting, is likely to be referred to as abuse. Why should this be so? Perhaps one reason is that by renaming rape as 'abuse' in such circumstances we hope, in however sublimated a way, somehow to sanitise this most awful of acts. It is almost as if we hope to circumvent the feeling of revulsion that we might experience if we allowed ourselves to contemplate the possibility of anyone transgressing the yet-to-be-named taboo against younger and fitter people imposing sex on elderly and possibly frail people. It is almost as if by referring to such heinous acts as 'abuse' we can avoid having to acknowledge and name this taboo.

Sexual abuse can be viewed as encompassing not only all kinds of sexual assault, including rape, but also other species of act in which one person sexually misuses another or others, even where the use of the term 'assault' would be inappropriate. To our mind the term 'sexual abuse' should be used to encompass sexual assault, which by its nature involves violent bodily contact, and also other forms of sexual misuse of others that do not. Abuse that does not involve assault is usually divided into two categories, 'contact' and 'non-contact' abuse, depending on whether the abuse involved touch. Both categories could be further subdivided. For example, non-contact abuse could be subdivided further on the basis of whether the abused person is expected to perform sexual acts or to watch sexual acts, and also on the basis of whether she is aware that she is involved in the abusive scene and, if she is, whether she is aware of its abusive character.

The territory mapped by the term 'sexual abuse' should, we think, be expanded to include sexual acts in which one person is used by another rather than related to as a person in the context of a relationship (or even a moment of relating) that is mutually fulfilling. So, for example, in any situation in which one or more people use another person or persons for sexual purposes when these other persons do not consent to being used in this way, sexual abuse will have occurred; this would include both contact and non-contact abuse. We would wish to include in the category of sexually abusive acts many acts which, when they take place between otherwise consenting adults, would be considered perfectly ordinary by many people. This would include occasions where one person thinks that what is going on is love while the other person knows that it is nothing of the kind. Consider, for example, a story told by Fairbairn (1995) in a different context:

> consider two people holidaying in the same Florida hotel who have met, apparently by chance, but actually because one of them, in the best tradition of Hollywood movies, has set things up so that their meeting is inevitable. The one who has staged their 'chance' meeting has designs on the other and spends the evening flattering and wooing and generally setting the scene for a 'romantic' and intimate encounter. The other, romantically wooed and flattered, and melting with the passion that such wooing and flattery can produce, is persuaded after more flattery to 'have a nightcap' in his new acquaintance's suite. In this situation a seducer has used all available means to get another into bed. The seduced individual for his part construed his new lover's flattery as genuine and honourable interest; he has construed his companion's act – which is in truth not what it seems to be for s/he is acting the romantic while being a scoundrel – as a genuine expression of interest in him as a person. His companion's act is one of seduction; the flattery was designed to ensnare him. When he wakes up alone the next morning to discover that his lover of the night before has checked out of the hotel, he realises that rather than having been swept off his feet in the spirit of all true romance, he has been used, abused and discarded. As a result he will probably reconstrue his lover's actions as an act of despicable deceit. (pp5–6)

Many people will think us quaintly old fashioned to disapprove of the actions of the seducer in this tale. After all, you might think, we all know that things of this kind go on as a normal, if not everyday, part of adult life in the late twentieth century; as a result you might consider us prudish to think, as we do, that the seducer in the Florida hotel has abused his/her partner for the evening. Perhaps we should make clear that what we consider to be morally repugnant about this scene is not the fact that the seducer and seduced spent the night together doing whatever, as lovers, they chose to do. No, what we disapprove of is the way in which the seducer used her/his victim as an object through which to satiate his/her sexual appetite. The seducer in the Florida Hotel uses the fact that her/his victim is *vulnerable* in some way to ensnare him/her into sex. And couldn't we all name a wide range of human conditions that might make a person hungry for love (that is, for old fashioned loving care) and hence vulnerable to romantic flattery? And someone who abuses a person with learning difficulties, whether by seducing her or by forcing himself on her, and whether or not the abuse involves physical contact, uses the fact that his victim is vulnerable in another way[9] in order to get his way with her. Both use vulnerable people as a means to sexual gratification. And both are, as a result, sexual abusers.

In our reconnaissance of the territory covered by the term 'sexual abuse', we have begun to identify features that characterise abuse as abuse. There is no one act, no one way of touching, watching, being with, relating to, or imposing on another person, that is sexual abuse. Sexual abuse consists of a family of acts: passive and active, involving and not involving contact, in which others are treated not in their wholeness as persons but as vehicles for gratification, where trust is absent and intentions are dubious. Although it is no easy task to move from recognition to definition, it will be worth looking closely at some attempts by others to do so.

Some attempts at definition [10]

Brown and Turk (1992) explain that their attempt to define sexual abuse is intended 'not only as a step towards collecting accurate information about current levels of reported abuse, but also as part of our commitment to practitioners to clarify the issues involved' (p.44). We are more interested in the second of these two reasons for deciding what abuse is. If a bad definition is decided upon, the collection of data will produce bad statistics and give unreliable indications of levels of danger. This could obviously have some effect on the organisation of services which could, in turn, affect the welfare of people with learning disabilities. More importantly, from our point of view, having the wrong way of thinking might mean that individual people are put at risk because those who should be caring for them will not have the correct conceptual spectacles through which to view, assess and make decisions about actions and behaviours that they see or that are reported to them. They might thus fail to spot and act upon evidence that abuse is taking place or might be taking place; on the other hand, they may spot abuse where none exists.

If too limited a definition is settled on, this could have the effect of excluding some behaviours that might otherwise be considered abusive, while if the accepted definition is too loose, this could have the effect of including into the category of behaviours said to be abusive some that were entirely innocent of blame. Thus, for example, if sexual abuse is defined solely in terms of physical contact, voyeurs of the kind exemplified by Peter Green would not be defined as abusers, though they might still be thought guilty of some other offence; nor would people like Charles's neighbours be considered abusers because their actions did not involve contact of any kind. On the other hand, if sexual abuse is defined solely in terms of touch, so that touching various bodily parts is defined as sexual abuse without reference to the state of mind or intentions of the individual doing the touching, then care assistants, medical practitioners and others who are involved in routine procedures of care could mistakenly be branded abusers.

There is a large literature discussing the kinds of things that might be thought sexually abusive. For example Brown and Turk (1992) cite Finkelhor's national survey about the prevalence of sexual abuse which included the following categories of abuse: 'actual or attempted intercourse; acts "involving someone touching you, or grabbing you, or kissing you, or rubbing up against your body either in a public place or private"; taking photographs, exhibitionism or performing a sexual act in front of you; oral sex or sodomy'. Brown and Turk (1992) themselves follow convention in dividing abuse into two types: non-contact abuse, which may consist of looking, photography, indecent exposure, harassment, serious teasing or innuendo; and contact abuse, which may range from touch, eg of breast, genitals, anus or mouth, to masturbation of either or both persons and penetration or attempted penetration of vagina, anus, or mouth with or by the penis, fingers or other objects.

We are unconvinced that it is necessary or even helpful to list specific behaviours in the way that lists of the kind we have cited do. For one thing, to list certain behaviours as abusive might suggest that other behaviours are not. If someone is capable of understanding at the kind of level that would make us inclined to consider him an abuser were he to act in certain ways, we do not think that it is necessary to tell him that it is wrong to penetrate another person's body with one's fingers, or penis or other objects if she does not consent to one's doing so, or to force someone to watch one performing sexual acts with another person. On the other hand, to list 'serious teasing or innuendo' as abusive might lead those who consult such lists to believe that milder forms of teasing and innuendo are acceptable and not abusive, whereas the question of whether such activities are abusive does not depend on their level of seriousness alone but on a number of other factors, including, for example, the intention of those involved and the effects on the individual who is the subject. In any case, who is to say whether teasing is serious or not? To be fair to Brown and Turk, they caution against seeing these factors as a hierarchy of severity in the absence of background information regarding the victim, the perpetrator and the social context in which the incident occurs.

Sgroi (1989) defines sexually offensive behaviour as:

one person's looking at or touching certain parts of a second person's body (breasts, buttocks, inner aspects of the thighs, or genital and anal areas) for the purpose of gratifying or satisfying the needs of the first person and when a barrier to consent is present for the second person. Sexual offense behavior may also include exposing one's genital area to another person and/or compelling that person to look at or touch the above mentioned parts of the first person's body when a barrier to consent is present for the second person. (p251)

Two points about Sgroi's definition demand comment. The first concerns the notion that there are certain parts of the body that are peculiar in being parts that it might constitute abuse to look at or touch. This is interesting because it does not allow, for example, that a person could take sexual pleasure out of touching parts that are not included on this list, some of which are less generally considered to be erotic – for example, forearms, ankles, 'outer aspects of the thighs', 'inner aspects of the wrists', earlobes, lips and hair – though it is not beyond the bounds of possibility that these might be a focus of erotic attention for some people. The second refers to the interesting notion of 'barriers to consent' which appears both in Sgroi's definition and in others. Talking of 'barriers to consent' seems to be another way of saying that there is some reason why the person who is abused cannot consent to acting in the ways that are required of him, whether this involves contact with the perpetrator or not, or to being used in the ways that the perpetrator intends and wishes to use him, again whether this involves contact or not.

According to Sgroi (1989), 'barriers to consent' may take a wide variety of forms including:

age less than 16 years; the presence of a parental, custodial or caretaking relationship between the persons involved; the use of a weapon, threat of injury, or use of force by the first person; the presence of a cognitive inability in the second person to understand the basic elements of sexual behaviors...or the presence of a power imbalance between them which precludes consent by the weaker person. (p251)

Sgroi seems to be making judgements about when it is realistic to expect that agreement between parties can be trusted to have been reached without either party feeling pressurised. We go along with the idea that the extent to which a person has agreed, willingly and with understanding, to his part in the kinds of sexual act that may be thought abusive can be important in coming to a decision about whether or not abuse has been experienced or perpetrated. However, it seems to us that to talk of 'barriers to consent' is to complicate matters. In addition it does not seem to us that some of the factors that Sgroi lists could be seen as barriers to consent, though thinking about them might make us take more care in assessing whether consent had in fact been given.

For example, the presence of a parental, custodial or caretaking relationship would not preclude the possibility of consent. A person could consent to having sex with someone who had been taking care of him for many years and might indeed be anxious to have sex with her. And, for example, presumably at least some occasions when a daughter goes off with her mother's new husband are examples of situations where a parental relationship has not prevented the younger person from consenting to do what she did with her parent's spouse. Age in itself does not prevent a person from consenting, though immaturity could mean that, whatever chronological age the person has attained, she does not know her own mind. Nor does it necessarily seem to be the case that, solely because there is a power imbalance between the parties, agreement of a consensual kind cannot be reached. No doubt many secretaries who have sex with their bosses, or students who are seduced by their lecturers, or other relatively powerless people who enter into sexual relationships with those who have power over them, are constrained into doing so, or persuaded to do so because of the nature of the relationship. However, there does not seem to be anything necessary about the fact that this must be so. It is conceivable that some such relationships may have been established on a mutually consenting basis, though this is not to say that there is nothing morally dubious about them.

We believe that the presence or absence of consent is important in coming to decisions about which acts are and which acts are not abusive. What is important is that in abusive situations where consent is an issue the person who is abused will not have consented to acting in the ways that she is expected to act, or to being used in the ways that the abuser chooses to use her. Whether she does not consent because she is unable to do so is in a sense irrelevant.

How should we define sexual abuse?

In trying to get to grips with the problems that arise when one attempts to arrive at a definition of sexual abuse, we have found ourselves frustrated by the limited and limiting nature of the language that is currently available to speak of the unspeakable. In some respects the problems one meets in trying to define sexual abuse are similar to the problems one would meet if one tried to give a definition of a game. There are games of many different kinds and these share a variety of features which knit them together as a family of activities which resemble one another (Wittgenstein, 1974). They do not share one set of characteristics, the presence of which together is necessary and sufficient to decide that a particular activity is a game. For instance, not all games involve the use of a ball, or a bat, though many do; and not all are played between two teams, though many are; not all are engaged in purely for pleasure, or have rules, or utilise a flat area called a game board or pitch or court, or involve rolling dice or betting on the odds that the dice will yield a certain score. It is thus very difficult to give a clear definition of a game. Yet we can all recognise games when we see them. In a similar way, we doubt whether it is possible to give an unequivocal list of characteristics, the presence or absence of which will allow us to tell whether any episode of human behaviour amounts to, or does not amount to, sexual abuse. And yet paradoxically we are inclined to believe that, like games, sexual abuse is easily recognisable.

We have not attempted to define sexual abuse by offering a list of activities, of parts of the body that might be touched and ways in which they might be touched, or of things that the abused person might be required or requested or encouraged to do, that would mean that another person or persons was or were abusing her. Our approach to definition has been more discursive. Throughout Part Three, and indeed elsewhere in the book, we have tried to display something of what we believe about the nature of sexual abuse – about what it is and how, for example, one might tell that a particular act is abuse and not something that just looks a bit like abuse. Our approach to saying what sexual abuse is, is less specific than that adopted by many other writers and does not rely at all on a description of bodily parts and what they can be used to do or have done to them. This may be thought unhelpful by some who work with people with learning difficulties. After all, it does not offer staff or services any 'rules of thumb' or easy prescriptions for assessing the meaning and effect of possibly abusive behaviour of which they have become aware, or which they have reason to suspect might be going on.

We are pessimistic about the possibility that definitions can be drawn up which would allow us easily to categorise acts of suspected abuse into those that do and those that do not constitute abuse; and to decide in relation to people who are suspected of abuse which are, and which are not, abusers; and in relation to people who may have been abused whether they have been abused or not. Nevertheless, we have attempted to develop some definitions. Those we have constructed include, within the phenomenon of sexual abuse, occasions when one person uses another person sexually when there is some disjunction in understanding or belief about what is going on between them and about which the abuser is aware, as well as occasions when there is an imbalance in power. We thus include in the category of sexual abuse some acts that occur between otherwise consenting adults. This way of thinking about sexual abuse, in which even the rogue in the Florida hotel would be considered an abuser, may seem unusual and as a result we expect that our attempts at definition might be found uncomfortable by many people whose behaviour at times will qualify as abusive when they thought that it was fairly run of the mill. After all, our approach to the definition of sexual abuse does not allow for the fact that at times most people are overtaken by lust and are less focused on relating to another with whom they have intimately engaged, as a person, than they might be. But whereas this might be a feature of the expression of sexuality for most people some of the time, in sexual abuse it is centrally important. The abuser never has good intentions towards the abused person in acting abusively towards her; this is not to say that he does not care for her, only that in this encounter what care there is, is overwhelmed by other desires.

We invite you now to consider the following attempts[11] at definition.

SEXUAL ABUSER

A *sexual abuser* is someone who aims at using another living and present person (referred to below as 'the subject') as the means to his or her own sexual satisfaction without regard for the other as a person with his or her own needs and wishes, if one or more of the following is also true:

— the abuser stands in a caretaking relationship to the subject of his or her abuse;

— the abuser is aware of the fact that sexual acts between him or her and the subject are prohibited, for example, by taboo;

— the abuser exerts power over the subject which is used to induce, persuade or force the subject into sexual acts in which he or she would not otherwise engage;

— the abuser deceives or attempts to deceive the subject into believing that what is taking place between them has a meaning that induces the subject to participate in acts aimed at his or her (the abuser's) own sexual gratification, or is aware that the subject has this belief and takes advantage of it;

— the abuser takes advantage of vulnerability (real or supposed) of some kind to gain sexual advantage with the subject;

— the abuser is aware of unwillingness or lack of agreement on the part of the subject.

SEXUALLY ABUSED PERSON

A person is sexually abused if, without his or her consent, another person involves him or her in activities aimed at their own sexual gratification. Agreement and consent are not the same thing and a person may be abused even if he or she agrees to participate in the acts or activities in question. Consent implies informed understanding and failure to consent may thus arise in several ways:

– because the abused person did not wish to be involved.

– because lack of understanding and/or knowledge, meant that the abused person was unable to consent.

–because no attempt was made either to consider the abused person's wishes or to respect them.

A person will also be sexually abused in most circumstances in which he or she has a sexual relationship with, or engages in sexual acts with, another person, when age or intellectual level and/or a caretaking or professional relationship means that a significant difference in power, status or level of understanding exists between them. A person in such circumstances may be abused even if the other has not made use of this differential to persuade or coerce him or her to engage in sexual acts or in a sexual relationship.

In some but not all cases in which a person is sexually abused, the perpetrator of that abuse will be an abuser.

SEXUAL ABUSE
Sexual abuse may be defined with reference either to the acts of an abuser or to the experience of an abused person. Whenever, in accordance with the above, a person is sexually abused and/or a person sexually abuses, *sexual abuse* will have occurred.

Why is sexual abu112se sometimes ignored and unreported?

Turk and Brown (1992) assert that at least 830 adults with learning difficulties are likely to be reported as victims of sexual abuse in England and Wales each year. It is a matter of ethical concern that the sexual abuse of adults with learning difficulties has only relatively recently been reported with any regularity since, in the absence of any reason to think otherwise, we may presume that it has been going on for a very long time. We might ask why this has been the case. Similar questions have been asked in the last twenty years or more, in relation first to the widespread physical and later the sexual abuse of children, and more recently in relation to the harrowing notion that elder abuse and yes, *elder sexual abuse,* may be common.

There are a number of possible reasons why sexual abuse may go undetected, unacknowledged, unreported and unacted upon.

First, it may go unnoticed because as a society we have absorbed some of the disablist myths and misconceptions to which we referred in Part Two including, for example, the idea that people with learning difficulties are asexual beings and so would not be expected to be involved in sexual encounters. Another related reason depends on the fact that people with learning difficulties are stereotyped as being physically unnattractive and often as having undesirable mannerisms and ways of behaving. As a result many people would find the idea of having sex with someone with learning difficulties so repulsive that they find it difficult to believe that anyone would want to do so. This fails to take account of the fact that even by common standards of physical beauty it is simply not true that all people with learning disabilities are physically unattractive. It also fails to take account of the idea that sexual abuse of any kind is largely about power rather than about physical attraction, romance or any of the other factors that typically contribute to the wholeness of willing sexual encounters. It is worth noting that similar reasons might be pinpointed for the failure to acknowledge the possibility that older people might be sexually abused, far less the idea that it might occur at any significant level. As already suggested, elder abuse of any kind has until recently been largely ignored, and the idea that relatives or carers would sexually assault vulnerable older people is so repugnant to most of us that perhaps as a society we have willed the existence of elder sex abuse, including rape, out of our communal imagination.

Second, it may be possible that the myths referred to above and in Part Two have such an influence on societal expectations that abuse has not in fact been undetected but rather has gone unremarked. Awful as it might be to stomach, people with learning difficulties might be considered to be of such little value in society in comparison with regular people that their abuse has been, and may still be considered to be, less serious than abuse of other citizens.

Third, those who have become aware that sexual abuse of people with learning difficulties was going on, or have suspected that it might be going on, might for some reason have chosen to avoid confronting the problem, perhaps out of embarrassment, perhaps out of fear of the repercussions. We are thinking of situations of the kind raised earlier, in reflecting on the possible meanings to be attached to the way in which the staff in his hospital failed to do anything to stop David's abusers. We are thinking also of occasions where abuse has occurred or is occurring in a service setting and the perpetrator is a staff member. In such circumstances, the perpetrator's colleagues may have persuaded themselves, somehow, that the individual or individuals with learning difficulties that they at first feared might be being abused were actually willing participants, perhaps even that it is good for them to have ordinary 'loving' relationships. It could even be that in circumstances such as these an abuser could persuade himself to believe this rationalisation, perhaps even believing that by having sex with his charges he was helping them to lead more normal lives.

A fourth reason that sexual abuse might go unreported and unacted upon, particularly in larger institutional settings, follows from the belief that it is better to allow sexual promiscuity amongst residents, even where this is not mutually fulfilling, than to stop it and risk the violent outbursts and consequent damage to people and property that can result from sexual frustration. In other words, sometimes staff may fail to intervene in sexual abuse between users in order to avoid the inconvenience that might result. If this is true, and however distasteful it is likely that sexual assaults on one resident by another are at times ignored for this reason, it is unacceptable; those who could have intervened to prevent harm, but did not, are guilty of allowing that harm to come about.

We find it is difficult to believe that staff might choose to ignore sexual assaults because they are concerned about the difficulty of dealing with any violence that may ensue. Serious violence amongst the residents of both large and small institutions is considered a grave matter by staff and it is unlikely that it would be left unchecked when it occurs. Certainly the staff in the institution where David lived would not have ignored the routine and regular assaults on him if they had been purely physical in nature. Physical violence demands immediate action in order to avoid injury, and though it may be a continuing feature of the relationships between some residents, it is also fairly clear what must be done in order to prevent injury and even in order to calm situations down. Many staff are able to respond swiftly, with skill and confidence, in situations where they suspect that physical violence is being or has been perpetrated on one resident by another or others. In contrast to this, staff are often less sure what to do about sexual abuse and in particular about sexual violence. It thus seems more likely to us that staff might fail to intervene in sexual abuse both because they feel that sexual activity is normal behaviour in their particular setting, and because they believe that since the results of sexual abuse are less noticeable than the results of physical violence, dealing with it is a matter of less urgency.

Finally it is perhaps the case that sometimes when abuse is reported in services, managers fail to act either directly or through the legal system because they have swallowed the myth that, by definition, people with learning disabilities cannot make credible or reliable witnesses. A person with learning disabilities who has struggled with and faced up to the enormous personal challenge of disclosing that they have been abused may then face further difficulties in finding someone who is not just willing and able to listen but willing and able to do what is right in the face of procedural or legal obstacles or the expectations of colleagues that it would be best to avoid the publicity, scandal and trauma.

As a result of the obstacles that might be put in the way of those victims who attempt to report abuse, some individuals may carry the scars of their experience for many years. This leads us to reflect on the need to provide people with learning difficulties with opportunities to share their concerns in ways and in settings that inspire confidence that they can expect to be believed and listened to. This is essential not only so that abuse can be detected as early as possible, but also in order that people with a learning difficulty who have been abused can be enabled to develop their credibility as witnesses should cases come to court. Consider Norrie, who was a leading light in a local self advocacy group.

> Despite his important position within the group it was some years after joining it that Norrie felt able to confide in the group advisor that he still felt upset and guilty about events in hospital more than two decades before when he had been regularly raped by members of nursing staff. Norrie's experiences of abuse at the hands of those who should have been caring for him were intolerable and caused him great harm, but what is perhaps worse is that in addition to the suffering that he went through at the time, many years later he had still not found a way of telling anyone what had happened and thus sharing his distress. His suffering and discomfort were further compounded by his obvious concern about the possibility that even now others like him were being abused by those same people.

Norrie's abuse came to the attention of workers only as a result of the opportunity and the encouragement to speak out that he received by being in the self advocacy group. His achievement in being able to disclose what had previously happened to him is not merely a matter of his having become more articulate, it is also that, having been in a social situation where assertion of one's rights is the order of the day, he had developed the self confidence necessary in order to be able both to share his experiences and to present and explore his views about them. One of the major objectives of self advocacy groups is to provide their members with the support they need in order to claim their rights, and it may be because self advocacy groups are increasingly recognised by users as a context in which they will be listened to and believed, in which their experience will be accepted and validated, that they attract people with learning difficulties who have been abused. One self advocacy group advisor has told us about his belief that most committee members in the group that he supports have at one stage or another been sexually abused. That this should be so gives pause for thought about the extent to which services fail effectively to deal with the trauma that people with learning dificulties experience as the result of abuse. It also gives pause for thought about the extent to which the safety and trust engendered in an independent self advocacy group could and perhaps should be made universally and uniformly available within services if people with learning disabilities are not only to be cared for but cared about. Unless opportunities to share and to receive support are made available, users who have been abused will continue to be inhibited from disclosing the abuse that is experienced by themselves or others because of potential reprisals from those who abuse; and they will continue to carry the scars of abuse alone and without solace.

Notes

1 'Comment', *Community Care*, 29 October, 1992

2 Charles's story and Lillian's story are adaptations of examples discussed by Cullen (1992).

3 Details of this offence and a similar charge that may be brought under Scottish legislation are to be found in Ashton and Ward (1992).

4 All information about Mr Righton and his various friends and activities is drawn from the 'Inside Story' documentary, except what we say about his contribution to the book *Perspectives on Paedophilia* (Righton, 1981), which we have read with interest.

5 In law there are prohibitions on male members of staff or managers in hospitals or nursing homes (or in Scotland any accommodation provided by the Local Authority) from having sexual intercourse with a woman user of those services. There are no equivalent offences for female members of staff (Ashton and Ward, 1992).

6 We might reasonably expect that managers would ensure that male staff are fully informed of the provisions of those aspects of the law referrred to above which make it an offence for male staff to have sexual intercourse with users of hospital, nursing home or hostel/supported accommodation. For details of the legislation covering these offences see Ashton and Ward (1992).

7 There is some similarity between this idea and the rather contentious and perhaps dangerous idea that might be put forward that in certain cases where a woman has gone through an experience that may accurately be described, from her point of view, as 'rape' – because a man has had sex with her against her will – it would be innaccurate and unfair to say of the man that he was a rapist. This is not the place to unpack this idea fully but we should say that it rests upon the belief not that there are rapists who are innocent of harm but that there might be a small number of situations in which a man, for whatever reason genuinely believes that what is going on between himself and a woman who experiences his actions as rape, is mutually fulfilling.

8 It is worth reflecting also on the possibility that if David did enjoy the contact he had with these men, the reason for this might have been that he was being abused in another way, by being so understimulated by his environment that any stimulation was welcome.

[9] Or perhaps in both ways because a person with learning difficulties could be doubly vulnerable if, for example, she had been unlucky in love and was, so to speak, 'on the rebound' from a failed relationship.

[10] In thinking about the problems of definition we have been more concerned with the effects of abuse on people than we have with punishing those who abuse, and it is because of this that we have steered clear of detailed discussions of legal definitions. Many sexual acts are legally allowed and carry no penalty for those who enact them, yet are damaging to people. On the other hand, some acts that are legally prohibited are not necessarly damaging to those who, legally speaking, would be thought to be victims of them. Cases in point here would be acts in which homosexual men might engage when they are under the age of consent for homosexuals but in which there is mutuality and self regard, and also those in which heterosexual people might engage when they are below the age of consent for heterosexuals, in which there is both mutual and self regard. In citing these as examples of illegal acts which are not necessarily harmful, though they are illegal, we do not wish to appear too liberal on this matter; indeed we consider that there is a strong likelihood of harm coming to those who become sexually active at too young an age, whether they are homosexual or heterosexual in orientation. However, we recognise that people mature at different rates both physically and emotionally and hence that they will be ready for and able to make positive use of, or cope with, sexual relationships with others at different ages.

[11] It is important to note some additional points in relation to our definitions:
  i. Sometimes a person will be the subject of sexual abuse but not be abused, and sometimes a person will be a perpetrator of abuse that is experienced by another person without being an abuser.
  ii. For abuse to have ocurred, harm need not be present in the abusive act. Likewise a person may abuse another without harming him or her, and a person could be abused without being harmed.

PART FOUR

Being and becoming: sex education, responsibility and the limits of inclusion

We have argued that people with learning disabilities have the right to know about sex, to enjoy sexual activities on their own, to have sex with others who wish to have sex with them, to have ongoing relationships of a sexual kind, to marry and to found families. If we value sex and sexual relationships, and we value people with learning difficulties, then our reasons for informing and educating them about sex should at least partly be focused on the joy and pleasure (even fulfilment) that they might thereby be enabled to obtain. In spite of this, negative rather than positive factors tend to be high on the list of reasons for sex education with people with learning difficulties.[1] Indeed, the dominant ethos within services is concerned with protection rather than with enabling informed, even *responsible* decisions about whether, how, when, where and with whom, to enjoy sex.

Certainly, many people with learning difficulties are likely to be more vulnerable to exploitation and abuse than their regular contemporaries because the chances are that they will be less well informed, less worldly wise and perhaps also less assertive. Everyone should know about sex and should learn about sex in ways that do not cloud the issues; young people with learning difficulties, just as much as their regular peers, should at least know enough about it to be in a position to decide not to do anything with their bodies that they do not want to do. In order to ensure at the very least that they can avoid entrapment into situations where they are sexually abused, it is thus important that people with learning difficulties be offered support, information and perhaps advice, in a way and at a time that is appropriate to their age, stage of development and level of understanding.

Everyone should have the opportunity to receive comprehensive and well-balanced sex education. More than that, in our opinion all pupils in schools should be *given* sex education and not merely the opportunity to receive it; in other words, in the same way that other important areas like maths and science and language are compulsory subjects, we believe that sex education should be a compulsory subject within all schools. Sex is not like religion, and we do not consider that parents should have the opportunity to withdraw their children from sex education. Although we realise that we might be open to criticism from both liberals and conservatives, who for quite different reasons might believe it is wrong to enforce sex education on children no matter what their parents' views are, we want to insist that sex is such an important area of life that all citizens should be properly informed about it[2].

It may be possible to argue that parents and guardians should be able to influence the ways in which their children spend their time and gain enjoyment and fulfilment, and there might thus be cogent reasons for allowing them to withdraw their children from positive aspects of sex education in the same way as there might be cogent reasons for allowing them to decide whether their children watch TV or listen to certain kinds of music. However, there are no cogent reasons for allowing parents to withdraw children from aspects of sex education that may help them avoid distress or risk. If parents are entitled to withdraw their children from all or part of the sex education that is provided, this could mean that pupils (and, most importantly, those who because of their learning difficulties are especially vulnerable to abuse, or to other dangers that might arise if they are ignorant about sex) may be denied access to information that could protect them.

Although we believe that sex education should be compulsory for all pupils, it is important to emphasise that it should be appropriate and should take account, for example, of age and stage of development. In particular it is important that there should be no imposition of information that an individual is not ready or able to understand. Graham's story, which we discussed in Part Two, provides one example of the way in which the provision of sex 'education' that does not match up to the needs of the individual can be unhelpful and possibly damaging.

Not everyone agrees that all young people with learning difficulties should automatically be given sex education. Consider, for example, some of the stories from Part Two, including those about Jane and Irene, whose parents have never allowed their daughters to participate in such work. Many parents who try to keep their children away from sex may disapprove of sex education in any circumstances. They might do this for a variety of reasons, though the reasons Irene's and Jane's parents had might be considered typical; they were worried that involvement in sex education could encourage promiscuity not only in their daughters but, perhaps more worryingly, in the boys at school. Parents who share this point of view may argue that young people like Jane and Irene will never be ready or able to understand about sex and that this is why it is wrong for them to be given sex education. We reject the idea that informing people about sex and sexuality is likely to lead them towards promiscuous behaviour and we are not alone in this view. For example, Conneally (1988) argues that there is no evidence either that sex education encourages people with learning difficulties to engage in more sexual activity than they would otherwise engage in, or that withholding information about sex will deter them from participating in sexual activity.

Rather than having less need of sex education than their ordinary peers, as Jane's and Irene's parents and many others believe, we would argue that young people with learning difficulties actually need more advice and education in this area. Apart from reasons that relate to the belief we have already expressed that knowledge about, for example, pregnancy, the possibility of disease and the dangers of abuse, can lessen the dangers such youngsters may face, there are other reasons that are less dramatic but no less important. It is, for instance, vital that children with learning disabilities are aware of the consequences of behaving in socially unacceptable ways in order that they can avoid the strong negative reactions and hurt that might follow such behaviour. Children without learning difficulties are expected to respect the unwritten rules about appropriate behaviour in public places. As a result, they are told from an early age not to talk to and cuddle strangers; and they are soon informed about private and public parts of the body. Why is it therefore that we do we not have the same expectations of children with learning difficulties? Why do we so often assume that people with learning difficulties 'can't help it' when they behave in sexually embarrassing ways in public, rather than concluding that they just haven't been helped to learn what behaviour is okay and what isn't? Certain ways of interacting that were acceptable when they were younger will be less acceptable as they grow up and they have to be taught this. For example, it is important that young people with learning difficulties should not develop the idea that it is appropriate to embrace any adult they meet; and yet behaviour of this kind is not only common but is often encouraged.

Learning to make choices

Sex education must be placed in a context that is much wider than awareness of bodily functions, reproductive biology and the mechanics of sex. Given that in part it is designed to enable responsible and thoughtful choices, it should be related to the development of skills in making informed choices across all areas of human experience.

Learning to make decisions and to take responsibility for them is not easy and decision making of a simple kind needs to be worked on and developed as early as possible with all children, whether or not they have learning disabilities. If they are to develop as autonomous people in so far as they are able to do so, children need to be encouraged to make choices about everyday things as early as possible. If we do not give such choices early on in life how can we expect them to make decisions in adulthood? If you have never been given the opportunity to choose between orange juice and milk, between your red jumper and your blue one, between whether to have toast or bread with your jam, how can you ever be expected to make choices at a more complex and emotional level? And unless and until they are experienced in making simple decisions about their lives, there seems little point in trying to enable people with learning difficulties to be aware of and make the complex moral and emotional decisions that surround the experience and expression of sexuality. Clearly those who support the idea that people with learning difficulties have the right to live lives in which sex plays a part have a concomitant responsibility to ensure that sex education is offered in the context of education for decision making.

Typical children learn to make decisions and to take responsibility for them by being given the opportunity to choose in relation to a range of things – from simple to more complex matters – as they learn to be people. By contrast, many people with learning disabilities, both young and older, are denied the opportunity to develop skills as decision makers, even about simple matters.

There is more to becoming the kind of person that is able to make responsible choices in the area of sexuality than having been helped to develop the necessary skills and having been given the knowledge necessary to do so. Even when the need for education in decision making has been taken seriously, problems typically arise in relation to the opportunities that are necessary for choice to be exerted. There is little point in trying to enable a person to know her sexual needs and feelings and to be able to make informed choices about what to do about them unless at the same time she is able to make these choices in practice. For although sex education is more and more commonly thought to be not only a good but an essential thing, the provision of opportunities to put theory into practice is less likely to be taken seriously. This view gains some support from the findings of research that Davies and Jenkins (1993) conducted into the friendship patterns of sixty people with learning difficulties. They concluded that the social life of young people with learning disabilities is very different from the social life of their regular peers. Half the young people that they interviewed said that they had a special friend of the opposite sex. However, nearly all of these young couples found it impossible to develop their relationship beyond platonic friendship. Most people with learning difficulties are denied access to the resources that they need in order to exercise choice about the expression of their sexuality, including that most valuable resource – a safe but private space. And the lack of opportunities for privacy may be just as much of an inhibition to people in developing an intimate relationship as any lack of knowledge or lack of competence.

The lack of opportunity that many people with learning difficulties have to express and to enjoy their sexuality in acceptable ways raises many serious concerns of both a practical and an ethical kind. One of these concerns the question of whether, if they have the same right as anyone else to enjoy sexual activity and to form ongoing sexual relationships, there is a concomitant responsibility on the part of services to provide safe and secure private places in which they can do so. Most people with learning difficulties will be denied appropriate opportunities, both within service settings and in the home, to engage in sexual relationships with others. And the lack of private spaces in certain service settings – notably day centres and day schools – is arguably a prime factor in producing the range of problems connected with masturbation. In our experience this is one of the areas that causes most concern both of a practical and an ethical kind, for staff. This is a tricky topic and it is because it presents such serious ethical, legal and practical challenges to staff that we propose to look at it in some detail.

The expression of sexuality outside relationships

The problems masturbation creates for parents of people with learning difficulties and staff who work with them vary a great deal. They include the challenge of having to deal with teenage boys whose aggressive and sometimes violent behaviour is thought to result from frustration caused by the inability to masturbate properly, and the equally distressing and closely related problem of youngsters who engage in self injurious masturbatory behaviour. But there are also less immediately trying problems.

Dolores, a young woman with profound and multiple disabilities and challenging behaviour, constantly rubbed her private parts in public places. This disturbed both the staff of the day centre she attended and other users.

Antony, a teenager with severe learning difficulties, attended a special school. His teachers were even more upset by his obsessional masturbating than his class mates were.

What can and should be done about the offence that is caused to others by people who, like Antony and Dolores, are indiscriminate about when and where and in front of whom they masturbate? The problems in such situations include both the embarrassment that public masturbation is likely to cause and, for the individuals concerned, the effects that such behaviour is likely to have on others who find such behaviour distasteful, including the likelihood of rejection and name calling. This kind of behaviour will often be so embarrassing and upsetting for staff that, rather than attempting to deal with it, they will brush it aside until eventually a crisis forces them into dealing with it hurriedly and with a lack of adequate planning. Consequently measures that are taken may not be effective, and if they are effective they may have unwanted side effects. Consider, for example, the way in which the staff who were caring for Dolores chose to deal with her behaviour by placing a heavy table over the arms of her wheelchair, preventing her from masturbating when she was in the day room. Apart from the fact that by doing this they denied Dolores the stimulation and enjoyment that she gained from masturbating, preventing her masturbating did not take away the desire to do it but merely frustrated the possibility of fulfilling the desire; nor did it do anything to modify Dolores's behaviour when she did not have the heavy table over her chair. In reflecting on this course of action, the question arises whether it was designed to meet Dolores's needs or those of the staff.

Nor did the way that Antony's teachers chose to deal with him help in the long run, even though they were successful in modifying his behaviour so that it took place in private. They were pleased that after working at this problem with him over a number of months he began always to find a 'private place' in which to masturbate. However, although keeping Antony's masturbation out of public view was a definite advantage for the staff, it brought other problems because the mess he sometimes made in the toilet annoyed his classmates, who refused to use it after him and started to call him rude names. It is worth reflecting on the question of whether the staff who dealt with Antony really chose an appropriate place for him to engage privately in this pursuit. Lavatories, after all, are essentially public places and masturbation is essentially a private activity. Of course, in some settings, such as day schools or adult training centres, there will be little possibility of privacy; indeed this was so in Antony's case. But this does not lead naturally to the idea that teaching him to do his masturbating in the privacy of a toilet cubicle is the right way forward but perhaps suggests that the staff should have been working with his family in trying to teach him to confine it to the privacy of his bedroom.

More difficult to deal with than the kinds of problems faced by the staff who were working with Dolores and Antony are those that arise in relation to situations in which the inability to masturbate properly results in aggression. Consider, for example, the following story which we have discussed with many people:

> Jonathan, a seventeen year old teenager with Down's syndrome and severe learning difficulties, has no spoken language and very few signs. He is affectionate towards his teacher but is often violently aggressive to both people and property. At meal times he can be very disagreeable. Jonathan's teachers put much of his violent behaviour down to frustration. He spends a large part of each day rubbing himself against furniture and his teachers think that his violence is at least in part, caused by his inability to masturbate 'properly'. They believe that the best thing to do would be to give him assistance in how best to go about masturbating, but cannot work out how to do this in a 'safe' way.

In discussing this story with colleagues we have received a wide range of responses to the question of what might be done in a situation of this kind, including the following:

– 'He's got to be isolated from the other children to prevent him causing disruption to everything.'

– 'He could be given a sexual suppressant like Androcur.'

– 'He could be given some "girlie" magazines and sent off to his bedroom and left to get on with it.'

– 'He could be left in a room with a pornographic movie on the video.'

Isolating Jonathan from his peer group would do nothing either to analyse or deal with the problem faced by his teachers but would merely move it to another geographical location. And although giving him a sexual suppressant would reduce Jonathan's sex drive, it would not remove it altogether and might not totally curtail his distressing attempts at masturbation and his frustrated violence. In any case the question arises of whether the benefit such chemical treatment would bring, either to

Jonathan or to the staff or both, could justify the side effects he would suffer, even if it was only administered for a limited time in order to facilitate a longer term behaviour modification programme.

The idea that giving Jonathan access to pornographic magazines and movies could help him in learning to masturbate properly is absurd. In all probability he would just get more and more frustrated. Or at any rate he would become more and more frustrated if his sexual arousal was related to people and actions or events portrayed in such material. If it was and he still did not know what he had to do in order to relieve himself, his difficulty would be exacerbated by being given access to it. If, on the other hand, his arousal was not related to events and people portrayed in it, such material would not affect him at all. In any case it is worth noting in passing that the suggestion that 'girlie' magazines would feed his interests makes assumptions about his sexual orientation.

So what can teachers and others do for a boy like Jonathan? Let's look at another frequent suggestion about what could be done:

> 'Someone could show him what to do because he needs to be "taken in hand" literally – showing him how to do it properly, to climax.'

This way of expressing things is frivolous; however, this suggestion, which has been made over and over again in almost exactly these words, by colleagues with whom we have discussed Jonathan's story, offers probably the best solution to the problems he presents. It seems also to be the most ethical solution since it recognises that Jonathan has a need to experience sexual arousal and satisfaction as one of the benefits of life, rather than as a source of frustration. Unfortunately, given the risk of being misconstrued, it is also the most dangerous solution.

The idea that a professional carer or teacher might engage in sexually arousing activities with a person with learning difficulties raises many problems of both a practical and, more importantly, of an ethical kind. Practically speaking such a programme can only be implemented if someone is prepared to carry it out, that is, to lay hands on Jonathan to help him to learn and to practise masturbating until he can successfully bring himself to climax. Ethically speaking a wide range of questions arise in relation to the problems with which Jonathan is presenting his teachers, some of which are closely interrelated with practical and legal issues.

Consider, for example, the problems that are presented by the idea that a practitioner might engage in activities designed to sexually arouse a person with a learning difficulty, in order to help him or her to learn to masturbate, and, further than this, that she might even offer physical assistance to him or to her in doing so. This may be rather difficult to imagine because of the connotations of abuse that are brought to mind by such a practice, even though a person who acted like this because doing so was part of her duties in respect of the individual's programme would not be an abuser. We do not imagine every time a surgeon cuts open another person's body with a scalpel that he intends to do the kind of harm that a scalpel wielding murderer would; we trust that he is doing what is necessary to help his patient. So, in a case of this kind, it would be necessary to trust the practitioner and to view her role in terms, not of the actions that she is performing but of the reasons that she is performing, them; in terms, that is, of their meaning rather than simply their outward form. One way of thinking about the difference that meaning can make would be to utilise the distinction that Harré and Secord (1972) draw between the actions and sequences of actions that a person performs and the the acts that they represent. Fairbairn (1995) illustrates the distinction between *acts* and *actions*, like this:

> When I take a pen and write my name on a piece of paper, the sequence of actions that I perform can constitute a variety of different acts depending on the context in which I do so and the piece of paper on which I write. For example, I may be validating an execution, pledging money to a cause in which I have been persuaded to believe, or agreeing to make regular payments to a bank in relation to a loan which the manager has agreed to advance to me. (p.2)

And the action or action sequence that a person went through in masturbating a young man with severe learning difficulties or in assisting him in doing so could represent a number of different acts. It might seem to an uninformed outside observer that a sexual abuser and a professional person who had a role in the same boy's programme were doing the same thing by engaging in sexually arousing activities with a boy like Jonathan. However, the intentions of the protagonists (those who were doing the masturbating or assisting the other in doing so), the meaning of the behaviour, and the social context in which it was placed, mean that the act performed would be different in each case. In deciding whether they acted ethically it is the *acts* they performed that we should consider and not the sequence of *actions* they went through in performing them. At this level it is clear that a person who masturbated the boy for salacious and perverted reasons would have performed an act of sexual abuse. It is equally clear that a professional who performed the same action sequence with the sole purpose of helping him to know what it feels like to masturbate properly, and what he must do in order to induce this experience for himself, would be free from blame[3]. Nevertheless, the possibility that helping Jonathan or another person with learning disabilities to masturbate successfully might be frowned upon by many people, and even be considered abusive, would give good reason for staff who were involved in planning, managing and implementing such a programme to take great care always to record what was done, why it was done, who was present when it was done and other details. Keeping detailed records of work of this kind would always be necessary in order to stave off the possibility of criticism and even accusation, and to ensure that if such adverse circumstances arose there could be no reasonable doubt about the rightmindedness of what was going on.[4]

The unlikely but unfortunate possibility that a professional person assigned to the task might have a well disguised sexual interest in young men or boys (or women and girls, because similar work could be undertaken with them) means that an act of professional care and duty could at the same time be an act of abuse. This could never be wholly avoided, just as the possibility that an unscrupulous person could in other ways use his or her power and status to gain access to vulnerable others in order to satisfy his or her sexual appetites, could never be totally ruled out. However, it does give pause for thought about how decisions might be made about who should carry out such work.

Is it best undertaken by someone known or unknown to the individual in other contexts? Must the person who undertakes the work be somehow trained or qualified in this work? Must he or she be acceptable to the individual with whom they will be working? Should it be undertaken by a man or a woman?

We imagine that, for most people, the last of these questions would seem reasonable in relation to occasions when the young person with learning difficulties was male but wonder whether it would be thought reasonable in those (probably less frequent occasions) when she was female. We invite you to ponder on the reasons that we might have for imagining in this way, and whether they are justifiable and reasonable reasons.

Thus far we may have given the impression that only one ethical issue is raised by the prospect of a staff member in a school or social care setting giving practical help to a person with learning difficulties in learning to masturbate – whether it is possible that this could go on without being abusive. But even if we find it easy to accept that in such circumstances a professional person could rightmindedly engage in activities designed to sexually arouse a person with learning difficulties, there are other ethical issues that might arise in relation, for example, to the question of whether such work should be thought of as teaching or therapy or treatment, and the effects it might have on both the worker and the recipient. These are difficult questions to which we have no answers. The question of whether, in an individual case, such interaction between staff and users is either morally permissible, or personally and professionally wise, or likely to be pragmatically useful, must be for individuals and staff groups to consider, though reflection on the kinds of issues we raise might be useful in coming to conclusions about individual cases.

Other more tricky moral questions also arise which serve only to emphasise how dangerous, both personally as well as legally, this area is for anyone who becomes involved. For example, what if the person assigned to the task found themselves enjoying what they were doing with the youngster? Would this make them an abuser? Could such people continue with the task in spite of the discomfort that they felt about finding themselves enjoying it? Or would the fact that they did enjoy it mean that they should immediately ask to be excused involvement? What if asking to be excused this particular task led to damaging innuendo about them (or they believed that it would), or worse still that it led to disciplinary procedures against them, because by their own admission they had engaged in sexual activities with a client or pupil or user that they found enjoyable? What if, as a result of this contact, they found themselves craving further sexual contact with similar people? Who would be responsible for this development in a practitioner's character?

There are questions also to be asked about the effects of such a programme of treatment/therapy/education on the person with learning difficulties. One of these arises because of the possibility that by the kind of programme that we have been discussing it would clearly be possible to influence, if not the sexual preference of the individual concerned, then at least the gender direction from which he expected in future to find sexual satisfaction, because he might begin to associate sexual pleasure with the person who was assigned to the task. Aside from the possibility of influencing sexual orientation, there is the more general problem that might arise if the person with learning difficulties began to develop romantic feelings towards the practitioner involved in the work, which led him to attempt to reciprocate or to further develop what he took, in whatever way, to be a developing relationship between him and the staff member. This is a serious problem, especially for those who are committed to the idea that the proper place for sex is in the context of a loving relationship, and who perhaps believe strongly that sex education should be placed in the context of a consideration of moral values. What messages might a person with a learning difficulty who was being given such help take from the fact that a member of staff was regularly taking him to a private place to engage in activities of this kind? Clearly those who would engage in such programmes must explore the question of whether they are best carried out in a cool and clinical way or in a warm and friendly way. However, they will also have to take into account not only the ways in which either approach might be construed by others, but how it might affect the sexual and social development of the person in question.

Choosing a partner

We have argued that people with learning difficulties have the same right to. enjoy sexual activity and to form ongoing sexual relationships as anyone else, and we have explored the vexed questions that may arise if we are to implement the first of these supposed rights when the person is engaging in solo sexual activity in unacceptable places or inappropriate ways.

We want now to explore a little further the idea that people with learning difficulties have the same right to form ongoing sexual relationships as everyone else by considering the question of who they can expect to have sexual relationships with. For example, is it right to limit their expectations to include only people like themselves? Or do people with learning difficulties have the right to choose anyone they wish as a sexual partner provided that those they choose wish to reciprocate? Are there people with whom they cannot form sexual relationships because to do so would involve doing something that simply isn't done? The question we want to examine in detail is whether the risk of abuse means that sexual relationships between people with learning difficulties and ordinary people must always be prohibited.

The idea that people with learning difficulties might be able to have non-abusive sexual relationships with regular people represents a difficult moral hurdle. But should it? Is the possibility that two people who have widely differing intellectual levels might have a sexual relationship necessarily more shocking than that two people who are very different in some other way should have such a relationship?

We are all aware of romantic relationships in which there is a big difference in the ages of the people involved and some of us might even be living happily within such a relationship. We are exposed from time to time to stories about rock stars and film stars and politicians and media personalities who are romantically involved with people who are separated from them by generational age gaps. Though such stories are usually presented by the media in such a way as to shock, they are usually also presented in such a way that they titillate and entertain; as a result we have, as a society, grown to accept that the rich, the famous and the powerful have a right to engage in relationships of this kind, because the stereotyped ideas we have developed about their lives have led us to accept this kind of behaviour as quite ordinary. But we are likely to find the possibility of romantic or sexual relationships springing up between people whose ages are very different, surprising or even shocking when the people concerned are not rich or famous or powerful. Which of us has not come across or heard of relationships of this kind about which we have been inclined to be if not disapproving then at least quizzical?

When, as occasionally happens, a story is taken up by the press in which romance has flourished between a man and a much younger woman when neither is rich and famous, the relationship is likely to be presented as a curiosity. If, in addition to a large age gap, the female with whom he is having the relationship is under age, the man will be vilified and indeed he is certain, if the relationship is thought to be physical in nature, to be investigated and probably prosecuted. And of course, a man who is proven to have engaged in sexual intercourse with a girl under the age of sixteen will be deemed to have committed an offence and punished as a result.

It is clear that many people believe that girls of thirteen, and perhaps even younger, are able to make up their own minds what to do with their bodies, at least to the extent of deciding that they want to protect themselves against the possibility of pregnancy when they have already decided to have sex with a man. This certainly seems to be the implication of many of the arguments that were common in the UK in the unsuccessful campaign by Mrs Victoria Gillick of Wisbech in the early 1980s to achieve a legal decision to the effect that girls who were under age could not be prescribed the contraceptive pill without parental consent. At that time, many people of a so-called 'liberal' persuasion argued that under-age teenagers who wish to have sex have the right to protection against pregnancy, and that therefore even girls who are under age should be able to seek contraceptive advice and contraception without involving their parents. The ruling in the Gillick case allowed that a doctor was not always obliged to inform parents that contraception had been prescribed to a child under the age of sixteen, though this was only the case if the child had sufficient maturity to consent to contraception on her own (McKay, 1991).

And yet it seems likely that in relation to a case in which, for example, it was demonstrated that a forty year old man (let's call him Leslie) had been having sex with an eleven or twelve year old girl (let's call her Lisa), most people would believe not only that Leslie was acting criminally by having sex with Lisa because she was under the age of consent, but that he was guilty of the more serious offence of sexual abuse. However 'liberal' they are, or want others to think they are, most people are likely to think that, in such a case, what we have is a little girl on the threshold of adolescence who is having advantage taken of her by an older and wiser but decidedly wicked man. And this would be true even of those very 'liberal' people who believe that girls (or young women as they might call them) of this age have the right, with or without their parents' knowledge, to decide that they should use the pill because they have the right to make responsible choices about protecting themselves against the risk of pregnancy.

How do you react to the story of Lisa and Leslie? Perhaps you might like to think a little about whether your reaction would be different if the gap in their ages was a little less – if, say, Lisa was nineteen and Leslie was thirty three? What if they were fifteen and twenty nine respectively? Or fourteen and twenty eight? Or thirteen and twenty seven? Or eleven and twenty five? Or nine and twenty three? In each of these scenarios the age difference is exactly the same but there is a likelihood that our reactions are different. To most people the idea of a nineteen year old girl having a romantic involvement with a thirty three year old man would seem perfectly reasonable; indeed in relatively recent history a certain prince married when the age gap between himself and his future princess was very similar to this. However, when the same age gap is moved chronologically downward we tend to become less comfortable until by the time the woman is under the age of legal consent we are somewhat squeamish; and by the time we get down to an eleven or twelve year old girl having sex with a twenty five or twenty six year old man the idea that what is going on is sexual abuse is difficult to avoid.

How are we to tell whether a person is able to make a rational decision about whether she should engage in sex with another person? Is it sufficient that her image of herself is that she is competent to make her own decisions in the matter of personal relationships? Thinking about the possibility that people under the legal age of consent might become sexually involved with older people, it certainly seems clear that the fact that a young person believes that she knows what she is doing does not mean that it is necessarily the case that she is not being abused by the older person. Turning to the possibility of relationships between people with learning difficulties and ordinary people, it certainly does not seem necessarily to be the case that just because a person with learning difficulties has the same right to marry or form ongoing sexual relationships as any other citizen, she is competent to decide either in general, or in a particular instance, whether she should have sex with another person either on a one-off basis or as part of an ongoing relationship. Having the right to something does not necessarily imply that one is competent to decide whether one should take advantage of whatever it is to which one is said to have a right. However, it cannot be the case that just because a person is judged incompetent to make decisions of this kind she should not be afforded that right, or should have it withdrawn from her.

What happens if a person with learning difficulties has different expectations from those held by other people in her life about her ability to decide whether it would be in her best interests to begin a sexual relationship with another person? What should guide the way in which her future unfolds if there is a divergence of perceptions and her view of her ability to make such a complex moral judgement is different from that held by her parents, or her social worker, or her priest, or her next door neighbour, or her workmates, or anyone else? They may see as manipulative and abusive a relationship that she sees as perfectly reasonable, or they may see a relationship between two people as being doomed to failure simply because one of them is less able than the other.

Consider, for example, the following story

> Liam was a good looking young man in his early twenties who had attended a school for children with learning difficulties though he now held down a full time job as an assistant in the laundry at the local general hospital. His good looks made him very attractive to younger female staff and as a result he had a number of relatively brief sexual relationships over the years. One such relationship resulted in the young woman in question becoming pregnant. When Liam heard about this, he went to Vanessa and asked her to marry him. After some reflection, she decided that in spite of the fact that he was a bit slow, she would say 'yes' to Liam's proposal; after all, what he lacked in brains he made up for in good looks and gentleness. Ten years later they were still married, had two children and were living happily in their own home.

Lots of people were pessimistic about the possibility that Liam and Vanessa could make their relationship work because he had such a poor job and such poor chances of advancement that it seemed unlikely that he would ever be able to support Vanessa and the baby. The disapproval and upset that people felt when Vanessa and Liam got together, focused at least partly on the fact that they thought this couple could never make a go of things because it seemed likely that they would be in constant financial problems. However, it seemed also to focus on the idea that somehow it did not seem quite right that someone like Vanessa should go wasting her life with a man like Liam. Vanessa disagreed. Ten years later, living in their own home, she and Liam were still in love, still struggling for money and still enjoying their life together with their children.

In the next story disapproval was also strongly expressed but on this occasion the reason for the disapproval was quite different.

> Alice had lived in institutions since her early childhood. During her thirties she moved from voluntary residential care into a small local authority hostel where

for the first time in her life she took the opportunity to engage in a number of sexual relationships with men who were also resident in the hostel. All were short term. In this and many other respects Alice gained competence and confidence in herself. After some while she was able to move to supported accommodation where she made friends with people in the locality. In particular she became very close with Andrew, a retired widower with whom she began to have a sexual relationship. A short time later they set up home together and established a long term and ongoing relationship.

In spite of the fact that Alice and Andrew were very happy and seemed to be doing well together, community care staff who were supporting Alice in her new home when she left the hostel, expressed grave concerns about the wisdom of Alice's choice in beginning a relationship with this man who, they believed, was simply looking for a domestic servant to care for him in his retirement. During its early stages fears were expressed because the law seeks to protect women with learning difficulties from abuse by others by making it an offence for a man to have sexual intercourse with a woman whose learning difficulties are such that she 'is suffering from "a state of arrested or incomplete development of mind which includes significant impairment of intelligence and social functioning".'[5] Thus, in spite of the fact that he loved Alice, Andrew could have been deemed to be in breach of the law. Such was the measure of the anxiety that their knowledge of the law induced in staff that they engaged in actions designed to discourage a relationship that they knew to be right, because a blunt instrument of law declared it to be wrong; and the principal agenda in the eyes of staff and management became the avoidance of controversy rather than the fostering of happiness.

Though Alice and Andrew had a much harder time in establishing their relationship than Liam and Vanessa, in the end it was clear to most people who were involved in their story that the relationship was nothing but wholesome and beneficial to both of them. Indeed, not only did the staff who were supporting Alice eventually come to believe both that Andrew was well intentioned and that the relationship was good for Alice, but they became convinced that the law should be modified to take account of the fact that some relationships between couples, one of whom has learning difficulties while the other does not, are worthwhile and should therefore be supported rather than attacked.

In drawing what we want to say about the possibility of sex between people with learning difficulties and regular people to a close, we want to re-emphasise the fact that, in spite of the possibility of abuse and exploitation of people with learning difficulties by regular people, we do not believe that sexual relationships between these two groups are necessarily abusive or exploitative. Indeed, our awareness of real life stories like those of Liam and Vanessa, and Alice and Andrew, leads us to believe that it is entirely possible for two people with quite disparate intellectual levels to have a sexual relationship not because one is abusing the other but because they have fallen in love.

Finally, it is perhaps worth recalling a story referred to earlier in which a friendship that could have turned into a romance actually ended in disaster. We are referring to the story of Harry Chalmers and Lizzy in which, you will recall, Harry lost his job because of an incident in which he touched Lizzy inappropriately and in relation to which, you will also recall, we were inclined, along with many others, to have sympathy for Harry. In closing our discussion of the possibility of non-abusive relationships between ordinary people and people with learning difficulties, we would ask you to consider the fact that until the point at which the incident occurred (and indeed even after that point), the relationship between Harry and Lizzy was no less wholesome, no less affectionate and no less beneficial to the two parties than that between Alice and Andrew. The only distinction, and of course it is an important one, is that the relationship between Harry and Lizzy was a caretaking one, notwithstanding the fact that in this context real friendship had blossomed. We do not know how you reacted to this story but ask you now to reflect on whether your attitude to the relationship between Lizzy and Harry, and to the possibility that it could have developed into one where mutual physical intimacy played a part, might have been different had it developed like this after Harry's retirement, which was due only six months after the incident that ruined his life.

Long term relationships, parenthood and parenting

We have talked about the ways that people with learning difficulties become informed about sex and are supported in becoming sexually mature adults. We have talked also about the range of relationships that they might develop and have discussed the possibility that, although people with learning difficulties are most likely to have sexual partners who like themselves have learning difficulties, it is not out of the question that they might develop ongoing sexual relationships with, and even marry, partners who do not have learning difficulties. For most people the establishment of a long term committed relationship or marriage naturally raises questions about whether or not to have children. There is an assumption that if they want to have children they have a right to do so, as and when and if they please. But is this so?

- Are people entitled to be parents?

- If they are, will they be good parents?

- Will they at least be good enough, that is *adequate,* parents?

- How can we decide whether their parenting will be good enough, in order that we can judge whether they should be allowed or even encouraged to found families?

Some of these questions might seem a little odd. As a society we care about children. That is why we are appalled when we hear stories about children who have been abused, neglected, or even simply left 'home alone'. It is because we care about children that we are likely to feel supportive of any government or political party that professes to be in the business of protecting them and of attempting to ensure that they are nourished emotionally as well as physically. It is because we care that we are likely to believe that children should be removed from parents who have abused them or cruelly and wilfully neglected them.

As a society, and as individuals, we are used to thinking about how best children should be cared for and nurtured. We are used to making judgements about the parenting of others about whom we hear in the news; others who have neglected their children, who have failed to nourish them, even about those who seem to have failed to give their children moral guidance, to instil in them a sense of right and wrong. This may sound somewhat moralistic, but it is merely a reflection of society. Consider the kinds of things that people said around the time of the trial of the two young boys who were found guilty, in the UK, of the murder of James Bulger in 1993. In the attempt to explain the actions of these two young boys many people talked as if their parents were culpable, if not because they had directly influenced the children into wickedness then certainly because they had failed to give them guidance about the difference between right and wrong.

Questions about good enough parenting do not surprise us because we want children to be well cared for and well brought up. It is because we care about children that we are likely to feel sympathetic towards the idea that young people should be given help, even during their school years, in developing both parenting skills and the motivation to be good parents. However, the question of whether people are entitled to be parents is not one that in general we think about; instead it seems to be assumed that there is a natural right to parenthood.

But is there really such a right? Or is parenthood a privilege, something to which we should somehow be expected to earn the right?

Imagine how you would react to the news that the government had decided, as part of a campaign to get 'back to basics', that parenting skills were to be taught as part of the essential curriculum in schools. Not only that but that in future all prospective parents would be vetted by a new statutory agency, the *Parenthood, Parenting and Childcare Agency* (the PPCA as it would no doubt become known). If they matched up to the various measures of skill judged essential to adequate parenting, and if they demonstrated not only acceptable attitudes towards but the motivation necessary to fulfil the duties of parenthood, they would be granted a licence to procreate; if not, they would be denied a licence. Under the government's new system, at the onset of puberty, or shortly before, each child would have a long acting contraceptive surgically implanted. After the prescribed age for parenthood (invent your own) the individual would be entitled, on production of a parenting licence at a suitable hospital clinic, to have their implant removed. People who procreated without a licence would be open to prosecution. Possible sanctions would include the enforced removal of their child at birth, or its abortion before birth, and compulsory sterilisation both as a punishment for conceiving 'out of licence' and to prevent them from doing so again.

We have already suggested that most people are likely to be appalled by the dreadful abuse to which some children are subjected by their parents and carers. However, most of us would be just as appalled if the government decided to go beyond education and training for parenthood on the one hand, and punishment for those parents who abuse their children on the other, to instituting a system in which only those who were judged fit to do so actually had the opportunity of becoming parents.

Imagine how you might feel if some social worker or other agent of the state decided that since you were not matching up to the standards of parenting officially considered to be adequate your children should be taken to a place where they would be better cared for. If this were to happen you would probably feel as devastated as many parents (even those that we might quietly be inclined to believe were a bit inadequate) probably feel when decisions are reached to remove children on the grounds of neglect. And if someone decided that your skills and motivation as a parent were so lacking that steps should be taken to ensure that you would have no more children, you would perhaps feel that one of the most basic of your human rights was under attack. As a result, in spite of the extent to which, as a society, we value children and want for them the best of all possible worlds, the PPCA is an agency that we probably would not like to contemplate having a place in our liberal and caring society, because in our liberal and caring way we believe that parenthood is such a normal state that it should not be denied to those who wish to exercise their natural wish and ability to become parents.[6] But now consider the following questions:

- Are people with learning difficulties entitled to be parents?

- If they are, will they be good parents?

- Will they at least be good enough, that is *adequate,* parents?

- How can we decide whether their parenting will be good enough, in order that we can judge whether they should be allowed or even encouraged to found families?

We guess that these questions will seem less odd to most people. They will seem less odd because of the common belief that people with learning difficulties are unlikely to be adequate as parents because, not being very clever, they are unlikely to be able to do all the things that parents have to do, well enough to ensure that any children they had would flourish. To use the jargon of state agencies such as the PPCA, most people will probably believe that, as a general rule, people with learning difficulties are unlikely to be able to develop the competencies and skills and attitudes that go hand in hand with good parenting.

Generalisations about the nature of people are often rash because they are based on insufficient evidence. Consider, for example, the kinds of generalisations that are at times put forward about some groups of individuals – about, for example, men, who according to some women 'are all potential rapists'; or people from particular council estates, who some people in neighbouring areas may believe 'are all into petty theft and burglary'; or 'the young people of today', who are believed by at least some older people to be 'lacking in respect for authority and care for others'. Such generalisations about people and their attributes and aspirations are unhelpful and often not only misleading but simply untrue.

The assumption that people with learning difficulties make poor parents has led to negative stereotyping of parents with learning difficulties, based on less than secure evidence. It is an example of dangerous generalisation that helps to predispose us to accept actions that fail to regard people with learning difficulties as having the same rights as other people. For example, it has arguably contributed to the commonly held idea that non-voluntary sterilisation is acceptable in relation to people with learning difficulties as a prophylactic solution to the problems that unwanted children might cause, should the women in question become pregnant. We believe strongly that those who care about and can influence the lives of people with learning difficulties should guard against the possibility that they will be influenced in their actions by rash generalisations, both about the nature of parents with learning difficulties, and about the likelihood that people with learning difficulties who are not parents at the present time would be unable to cope with the demands of parenthood if they became parents at some point in the future.

Many people find it difficult to accept the idea of parents with learning difficulties. Even if the idea that they *could* be parents is accepted, at least in theory, the possibility that they might *in fact* be parents is likely to be regarded rather negatively. Writing about ethical issues in parenting by people with learning disabilities Brodeur (1990) goes so far as to claim that 'Problems arise because adults with mental retardation want to be parents' (p195). What are we to make of this statement? At one level it is obviously true, at least to some extent. Problems do arise because at least some people with learning difficulties do want to be parents, just as they arise because some regular people want to be parents. It is a fact about people that many of them want to have children; but it is also a fact that, however well planned and however fulfilling and enjoyable, parenthood is always demanding and often stressful, so that problems arise from the fact that people want to be parents.

Perhaps Brodeur simply wants to point out that in his view there is a higher likelihood that parents with learning difficulties will experience problems than that parents without learning difficulties will experience problems. If this is the case then he is correct to some extent. Certain demands of parenting including, for example, the need for detailed organisation both of resources, and more especially of time, require intellectual skills; and no doubt many parents with learning difficulties will find these especially demanding. But there are many parents who would not normally be described as having learning difficulties, who will also find these aspects of parenthood difficult at least some of the time. The authors of this book all fall into this category.

The stereotypical views of people with learning difficulties to which we have referred do not lead universally to the conclusion that they should not be permitted to be parents. Some people are drawn instead to the view that at least some citizens with learning difficulties should be allowed to become parents, but believe that this should only be permitted if certain criteria are fulfilled, including, for example, the requirement that the people with learning difficulties in question must somehow have demonstrated their aptitude for parenthood and show that they will make *good* parents, or at any rate that they will be able to provide adequate care, both physical and emotional, so that their children will not suffer. Despite their marginally more liberal views, such people will, nonetheless, want to place restrictions on the opportunities that citizens with learning difficulties have to become parents. What reasons might be put forward to justify this stance?

First of all, most people who are prone to the kind of rash generalisation described above are likely, in their ignorance, to believe that if people with learning difficulties become parents they will inevitably produce children who, like them, will have learning disabilities. They may take the view that people with learning difficulties should be prevented from procreating because they are likely to produce more children than other people, and thus to produce more children than they can adequately care for. If this were true, it would be regrettable, because it would mean more children who in the end would have to be cared for by the state. Finally, and most cruelly, they are likely to believe that the children of parents with learning difficulties are likely to be at substantially higher risk of neglect and even of abuse.

In justifying the view that where possible people with learning difficulties should be dissuaded from founding families and where necessary prevented from doing so, agents of the PPCA and similar organisations might point out that many people with learning difficulties are incapable of the simplest everyday tasks that are necessary in looking after children, even during the earliest stages of babyhood. In other words, it is likely that officers of agencies like the PPCA would take the view that people with learning difficulties are not only incapable of offering reasonable standards of care but would also be incapable of learning the necessary skills involved. Some advocates of people with learning difficulties who would wish to defend their right to become parents might point out that there is no reason why a person with learning difficulties should not be able to meet the first prerequisite of adequate parenting – that children be made to feel loved, wanted and valued. In reply, PPCA agents and others who agree with them might respond by pointing out that no child can feel valued and loved if its bottom is wet and it isn't being fed, arguing that people with learning difficulties are unlikely ever to be able to cope with feeding, bathing, nappy changing and so on. And even if they could be trained to perform such practical tasks in a routine fashion, it might be argued, they could not be relied upon to take responsibility for them or for any of the other practical tasks that go along with parenthood. This view is simply mistaken since, like their typical peers, some people with learning disabilities are able to develop the skills necessary for parenting, in spite of any deficiencies they might have. Consider for example the Raeburns:

> Both Jack and Edith had attended special schools themselves and all of their seven children attended or had attended similar schools. Despite this Mr Raeburn held down a job in the council cleansing department and he and his wife were well liked in the neighbourhood. Mr Raeburn routinely rose at five thirty not only to get himself ready for work but to ensure that his children

were fed, washed and dressed ready for school. Teachers at the school attended by Gordon, the oldest boy, frequently had to deal with outbreaks of head lice and, despite the best endeavours of Mr and Mrs Raeburn to assure them that they understood the procedures that were required and that they were making efforts to wash all of the children's hair with the medicated shampoo provided, Gordon was regularly blamed for bringing nits into school; as a result, on more than one occasion, he was subjected to the indignity of being sent to the de-lousing centre where he was ceremoniously cleansed.

The teachers at the school attended by the Raeburn children seemed to begin from the premise that people with learning difficulties are necessarily incapable of offering reasonable standards of care, and in particular that they are incompetent to deal with matters of personal hygiene. One of us was the Raeburn's social worker and was aware that Mr and Mr Raeburn not only fully understood but made special efforts to implement the necessary routine of washing the entire family's hair with medicated shampoo, combing with a special comb and so on, whenever there was an outbreak of headlice in the children's school. But in spite of both his reassurances and those of the Raeburns themselves, the predisposition to assume that because they had learning difficulties the Raeburns could not be adequate even in the matter of physical care, remained among the teachers at the children's school and also among members of his department.

In our experience, evidenced by the story of the Raeburns, it is likely that parents with learning difficulties will be viewed as incompetent even when they are not, and that as a result both they and their children may suffer at the hands of 'caring' organisations even in regard to relatively routine aspects of child rearing. Many parents with learning difficulties report that they feel themselves under scrutiny from the very start and that they live in fear that they will lose their children. Booth and Booth (1993) tell of one mother's anxiety:

> Apart from undermining her self-esteem and sense of worth as a mother, she feels under constant pressure to prove herself to others and that any mistake she makes may result in her losing the children. She dare not admit to her difficulties but strenuously denies them for fear of the consequences. (p.389)

Being a parent is, generally speaking, a valued role in our society but it is clear that for many women and men with learning difficulties it does not always result in their being bestowed with positive social value, even by agencies that subscribe at least nominally to the principles of normalisation or social role valorisation. Indeed, the status 'parent with learning disabilities' tends to become an all encompassing one and perhaps the only aspect of the person that the statutory and other services are interested in. Consider, for example, the Trotters, both of whom had learning difficulties and both of whom had grown up in care.

> Barbara had spent many years in a single sex institution run by a religious order, and even after she had left and set up on her own she tended to be reliant on the good will of the nuns to help her out of an occasional financial crisis. Stuart grew up in one children's home after another, usually moving on after his violent outbursts overstretched the tolerance of the care staff. In spite of continuing problems with their council flat, which is damp and is located in a depressing part of town a long way from the shops, the couple's two year marriage has seen them growing from strength to strength. They have developed reliance on one another rather than on support workers who have at times been burdensome in their interference. However, the level of attention from services increased considerably after Davey was born.
>
> Right now Barbara and Stuart are facing a crisis. The health visitor is concerned about unexplained marks on Davey's bottom. These concerns are shared by the social worker who believes that Davey should have been taken into care before now because people like the Trotters can't learn to look after babies, far less bring them up when they're older. When the professionals first raised these issues with them, both Barbara and Stuart denied that there was any problem really; privately they are terrified that Davey will be taken away, and their fears are justified. Care proceedings are now being considered by the professionals, who increasingly believe that it will be too complicated to provide the right level and intensity of support to the couple to make it possible for them to bring up their child in an acceptable manner.

No matter how well intended, taking recourse to a punitive and adversarial approach to parents who, like the Trotters, are experiencing problems in parenting seems to us to be mistaken. Obviously children have to be protected and we would not suggest that where there is doubt about their safety, social workers and others should leave them in situations where harm might come to them. However, in most circumstances, supportive intervention to aid people in learning to be parents is more likely to have positive effects on children's welfare. In relation to a couple like the Trotters, both of whom have learning disabilities and neither of whom was brought up in a settled nuclear family, support of this kind is even more likely to be needed and to make a difference. Yet the professionals involved with them have been anything but supportive and right now are quietly relieved that they have found some grounds (the unexplained and, if the truth be told, rather minor 'marks' on Davey's bottom) for pursuing action which may lead to his removal from his loving parents. In our view this would be unjustified and bad, not only for Stuart and Barbara but for Davey.

The difficulties that the Trotters face as parents are being compounded by other problems such as poverty, poor housing, victimisation and lack of support. It is ironic that men and women like them, who are doing their best to carry out the tasks of parenthood in conditions that would prove burdensome even for people without learning difficulties, should be criticised for failing, rather than attention being directed to ways in which services are failing them.

Those who maintain generalised and negative views about the idea of people with learning difficulties as parents, and hence of the prospect that they will found families, are not only misguided but morally mistaken in doing so. Typically, professionals charged with supporting such parents will claim that they perceive their job as being not only to support parents but more significantly to ensure the welfare of the children in such families. If they are to do their best not only by parents who have learning difficulties but by their children, they must avoid setting standards of capability and performance in terms of parenting that most parents would find hard to live up to, including many like ourselves who do not have learning disabilities. They must ensure that the difficulties faced by parents with learning disabilities are not made worse by services that are supposed to be supportive but instead actually undermine their confidence and restrict their opportunity to gain the real and lasting pleasure and fulfilment that so many of us achieve from this role.

Reprise: people with learning difficulties as sexual beings and parents

In this book we have addressed a few of the ethical issues that arise from the need to take seriously the question of whether it is right that people with learning difficulties should see themselves and be seen by others as sexual beings. We have addressed the question of whether it is right that they should engage in sexual activity and in long term sexual relationships either with people like them or with men and women without learning difficulties; we have explored the question of whether it is right that such relationships might lead to pregnancy and to parenthood and parenting.

In Part Four we have argued that if we value people with learning disabilities we will ensure that they are informed about sex in order that they are able to make responsible decisions in this area of life. We have also argued that a comprehensive programme of sex education should be provided for all pupils, while pointing out that there is little point in providing such education for young people with learning disabilities if they are subsequently denied any opportunity to express their sexuality.

To do so would be to treat them as passive sexual objects at risk from the predatory attentions of others, rather than as active sexual persons entitled to the joys and pleasures of sex and sexual relationships. It is, of course, right to be alert to the possibility that some relationships in which people with learning difficulties might engage may become abusive. However, it is futile, unreasonable and morally wrong to manage the risks associated with sexual maturation by keeping people uninformed or by undermining the possibility of them expressing their sexuality by placing constraints and obstacles in the way of their doing so. One such constraint to which we have drawn particular attention is the lack of the privacy which is necessary both for the development of intimacy in relationships and for other sexual activities, if these are not to cause offence to others.

If people with learning difficulties are given education, opportunities, support and respect by practitioners, parents and others, many of them can and will go on to develop and sustain satisfying long term relationships and marriages, either with other people like them or with regular people. Despite the negative stereotypes that surround us, some such couples, as we have argued, will not only choose to have children but will become successful parents. When such couples encounter practical and emotional difficulties as parents, we believe that well timed and well tuned support should be provided at least to the same extent as it is to all parents who encounter problems with parenting. However, even with support, some such couples will face continuing difficulties with parenting. In such circumstances we believe that it is crucial that practitioners should conceptualise the problems as lying at least partly in the nature and extent of the support arrangements provided, rather than retreating readily into sterotyping in which the problems are viewed simply in terms of perceived and imagined deficiencies of the couple. As we have shown, parents with learning disabilities are likely to be held to higher standards in terms of parenting than their ordinary peers, and at times imagined deficiencies that lead to unwelcome interventions on the part of services, stem from the predisposition of staff to expect to find them, rather than from evidence of actual deficiency.

We began our discussion of parenthood and of parents with learning difficulties by asking some questions about the rights of people to become parents and about how it is possible to decide that their parenting is what might be called 'good enough' parenting. In a society which supports those who need support, it is appropriate that parents with learning difficulties who need it should be supported in caring for their children. To conclude our discussion of parenthood we want to pose a further set of questions, though this time they do not focus on the rights of people with learning difficulties, but on the responsibilities of practitioners in support services:

- When and in what circumstances should services support people with learning difficulties in becoming and being parents?

- Will such support be good enough; that is, will the services that are provided be *adequate* support services?

- How can we decide whether they will be good enough and whether they are good enough, in order that we can judge whether they should be made more widely available to parents and potential parents, both those who have learning difficulties and those who do not?

Notes

[1] Most of what we have to say about sex education and related matters will refer specifically to children and young people with learning difficulties, though it will have relevance also for many older people with learning difficulties.

[2] Some people who are sympathetic to the view that all children should receive sex education would nevertheless argue against making sex education compulsory in school. We understand this view, in particular when it springs from a fear that teachers might make a mess of teaching children about sex. One person with whom we discussed this issue was adamant that she would rather take responsiblity for her children's sex education than give responsibility for this important area to some teachers she had come across. We share the fear that sex education might be badly and insensitively handled so that children are given misleading information, just as we fear that our children might be given misleading information in other areas of the curriculum. Nevertheless we still believe that sex education should be compulsory though we might be persuaded to make an exception in the case of parents who were able to demonstrate that they were providing adequate and appropriate education about sex at home, in the same way that parents who decide wholly to educate their child otherwise than in a school may be expected to demonstrate that the education they are providing is appropriate and adequate.

[3] It is worth noting that the physical actions involved in this kind of work might well be repulsive to the practitioner involved, in the same way that many personal care tasks performed in relation to those who are in receipt of physical care may at one level be found repulsive.

[4] Ashton and Ward (1992) offer detailed advice about safeguards that might be implemented when conducting sex education programmes where doubt could be raised about staff motives.

[5] This passage from section 106 of the Mental Health (Scotland) Act, 1984, cited by McKay (1991) is mirrored by similar provisions in the equivalent legislation in England and Wales.

[6] In referring to the exercise of the 'natural ability' to become parents, we are talking about the exercise of reproductive functions and fertility, rather than the ability to become a parent in the sense of the development of the skills, understanding and knowledge necessary for parenting. In other words, we are talking about *parenthood* as a biological function rather than *parenting,* which is a social, personal and perhaps spiritual role. It

is the ability to empathise with those who experience an intense desire to become parents that makes many people sympathetic towards the plight of those would-be-parents who are willing to sacrifice both financially and physically in order to become biological parents using reproductive technologies such as IVF, when for some mechanical or other reason it is difficult for them to do so by the usual means. Interestingly, one aspect of the PPCA that is already present in our society is to be seen in the controls exerted by clinics offering help of this kind to would-be-parents, and also in the criteria used by adoption agencies, where the choice of suitable candidates amounts, at least in part, to an assessment of their suitability as parents.

Endnote: a backward glance

Sexuality, Learning Difficulties and Doing What's Right may not be the book you expected it to be when you bought it, took it out of the library or picked it up in a bookshop and flicked through to the end in the hope of finding out what it is about. It is written in a storytelling rather than a documentary style. It is not a scholarly book, in the sense of being a detailed and sombre overview of its subject matter, firmly embedded in a detailed study of things that other authors have written. However, it has resulted from a great deal of thought over issues about which we feel passionately concerned and which are of enormous importance to those who are personally and professionally involved in them. In writing it we did not hope to present a body of received knowledge or even wisdom about the sexuality of people with learning difficulties. Hence we have not, as is the tradition in social science and educational research, undertaken a formal review of the literature – a wide trawl of what has been written in this area – though we have referred extensively to other work with which we were or have become familiar.

The book is not the result of empirical research; we have not based our reflections on long hours of structured and semi-structured interviews with people who have learning difficulties, or with their parents, carers or teachers. We have not based it on the analysis of numbers – of people with learning difficulties who are or have been sexually abused or have themselves been prosecuted in connection with sexual offences; who have settled down in long term relationships or marriages; who have had and reared children, or been subjected to involuntary treatment to avoid pregnancy; who have been divorced or had their child or children removed from them. Rather it has been based on reflection about personal experience and the shared experience of others, combined with the attempt imaginatively and empathically to enter into the lives of the people who inhabit the stories that we tell, whether they are real, true though not real, or wholly imagined.

Our intention has been to raise some issues about sexuality that arise in the lives of people with learning difficulties. The kinds of issues with which we have been principally concerned may be characterised as ethical issues: issues about right and wrong, good and bad, what should or ought to be done and what ought not to be done. Part of our intention has been to offer readers the opportunity to 'limber up' for the moral problems that they face, or perhaps for those that they try to avoid where possible because one reaction to moral problems is to distract oneself with 'practical' matters in the hope that questions of right and wrong will disappear. As we have tried to make plain, we believe that the moral problems with which we deal in this book are in themselves matters of immense practical importance, because the ways we think about them and the conclusions that we reach about them will affect the ways we act and the ways we live our lives.

We came to write this book because we were aware that, in spite of the fact that guidance is readily available about what *might* be done in relation to the sexuality of people with learning difficulties, people seem to be very unsure about what they *should* do, about what it is *morally right* to do. One aspect of the anxiety that they experience in this area concerns conflicts between what is expected by law and procedural guidelines, and personal feelings and intuitions about what is right and wrong. By creating a moral gymnasium in which most of the apparatus is focused on developing ways of thinking about sexuality and its place in the lives of people with learning difficulties, we have tried to make it possible for readers to to be better equipped when they face problems about what it is *right* to do rather than deciding what *might be done* or even what is required by statute, convention or procedural manual. 'Sticking to the book' in relation to legal and organisational requirements is a matter for those who can interpret rules, regulations and laws. For guidance on such matters you must consult legal texts that offer interpretations of the law, and other appropriate texts, including guidelines adopted by the organisation, agency or institution within whose system you operate.

We have tried to introduce you to some aspects of the moral territory in which practical decisions about issues relating to the sexuality of people with learning disabilities are embedded. Though we are wary of mixing our metaphors too much – after all, we have already created the idea of a moral gymnasium designed to help people limber up for life in the moral landscape we are addressing – it is perhaps worth thinking of this landscape as being somewhat like a maze. In mazes it is difficult to find one's way round because it is impossible to see where one is going. In a physical maze it is often difficult to communicate with others from whom one is separated by tall hedges. In the moral maze created by issues relating to sexuality and people with learning difficulties, the barriers are a mixture of difficulties caused both by different degrees of professional involvement and understanding and by differences in moral beliefs that have resulted from the contrasting ways in which we have been brought up both personally and professionally.

As we argued in Part One, there are no guidebooks to right conduct in relation to the sexuality of people with learning difficulties, and in writing a book addressing ethical issues in this area we have not tried to provide one. In attempting to enable people to find their way around the moral maze that thinking about sexuality and learning difficulties creates, we have not sought to delimit moral rules or even principles that are specific to this area of human life, though from time to time we have made our own views about particular problems plain.

Nor do we provide a map for the 'moral maze' that those who work and live with people with learning difficulties have to navigate when they are faced with the problems that arise in relation to sexuality. Maps are useful only in certain circumstances. They can only be provided when the territory has been fully explored; they are less useful when the territory does not have clear landmarks, as for example when traversing a desert; maps are often out of date very soon after and even sometimes before they are published. At this stage we do not believe that a moral map of the territory covered by thinking and action in relation to the sexuality of people with learning difficulties is possible, though we have at various points in the book offered sketch maps of smaller areas for consideration. Rather, by way of a number of stories from the lives of real and imagined people, we have tried to help you to gain an overall picture of the kind of territory you are in when you come to think about the moral questions sexuality raises. In doing so we have tried to illustrate how varied the landcape is. And by discussing individual stories and making some of their complexity clear, we have tried to help you develop your own moral sketch map.

Bibliography

Allington, C. (1992) 'Sexual Abuse within Services for People with Learning Disabilities', *Mental Handicap*, 20,2 (June 1992), 59–63.

Arras, J. and Hunt, R. (1983) *Ethical Issues in Modern Medicine*. Palo Alto: Mayfield Publishing Company.

Ashton, G. and Ward, A. (1992) *Mental Handicap and the Law*. London: Sweet and Maxwell.

Baker, P. A. (1991) 'The Denial of Adolescence for People with Mental Handicap: An Unwitting Conspiracy', *Mental Handicap*, 19 (June 1991), 61–65.

Barrie, J. M. (1911) *Peter Pan and Wendy*. London: Hodder and Stoughton.

Beauchamp, T. and Childress, J. (1994) *Principles of Biomedical Ethics*. New York: Oxford University Press.

Booth, W. and Booth, T. (1993) 'Accentuate the Positive: a personal profile of a parent with learning difficulties', *Disability, Handicap and Society,* 8(4), 377–392.

British Broadcasting Corporation (1993) Heart of the Matter *Hearts and Minds* (Screened 24/10/94: Roger Bolton Productions).

British Broadcasting Corporation (1994) Inside Story *Children at Risk: The Secret Double Life of a Paedophile* (Screened 1/6/94 : Producer Catharine Seddon).

Brodeur, D. (1990) 'Parents with mental retardation and developmental disabilities: Ethical issues in parenting'. in Whitman, B.Y. and Accardo, P. J. (Eds) *When a Parent is Mentally Retarded*. Baltimore: Paul H. Brookes.

Brown, H. and Turk, V. (1992) 'Defining Sexual Abuse as it Affects Adults with Learning Disabilities', *Mental Handicap,* 20,2 (June 1992), 44–55.

Campbell, A. (1972) *Moral Dilemmas in Medicine*. Edinburgh: Churchill Livingstone.

'Comment', *Community Care* (29/10/92), 13.

Conneally, S. (1988) 'Developing the sexuality of people with a handicap', in McConkey, R. and McGinley, P. *Concepts and Controversies in Services for People with a Mental Handicap.* Galway: Brothers of Charity Services.

Craft, A. (1983) 'Sexuality in mental retardation – A review of the literature', in Craft, A. and Craft, M. (Eds) (1983) *Sex Education and Counselling for Mentally Handicapped People.* Tunbridge Wells: Costello.

Craft, A. (1993) 'Parents with Learning Disabilities', in Craft, A. (Ed), *Parents with Learning Disabilities.* Kings Fund Centre, London: British Institute of Learning Disabilities.

Craft, A. (1994) *Practice Issues in Sexuality and Learning Disabilities.* London: Routledge.

Crain, L. (1980) 'Sterilisation and the retarded female', *Paediatrics,* 66(44), 650–651.

Cullen, C. (1992) 'The Sexual Abuse of People with Learning Difficulties', in Donnelly, P. and Nunno, M. (Eds) *Excellence in Training.* Dundee: University of Dundee/Cornell University.

Davies, C. A. and Jenkins, R. (1993) 'Young people with learning difficulties making the transition to adulthood', Social Care Research Findings, York: Joseph Rowntree Foundation.

Draper, H. (1991) 'Sterilisation abuse: Women and consent to treatment', in Brazier, M. and Lobjoit, M. (Eds) *Protecting the Vulnerable: Autonomy and Consent in Health Care.* London: Routledge.

Fairbairn, G. (1995) *Contemplating Suicide: The language and ethics of self harm.* London: Routledge.

Gillon, R. (1986) *Philosophical Medical Ethics.* London: Wiley.

Harré, R. and Secord, P. (1972) *The Explanation of Social Behaviour.* Oxford: Basil Blackwell.

Hollis, M. and Howe, D. (1987) 'Moral Risks and Social Work', *Journal of Applied Philosophy,* 4(2), 123–134.

Levy, S. R., Perhats, C., Nash-Johnson, M. and Welter, J. F. (1992) 'Reducing the risks in pregnant teens who are very young and those with mild mental retardation', *Mental Retardation,* 30(4), 195–203.

McCarthy, M. and Thompson, D. (1992) *Sex and the 3 R's: Rights Responsibilities and Risks.* Brighton: Pavilion Publishing (Brighton) Ltd.

McKay, C. (1991) *Sex, Laws and Red Tape.* Glasgow: Scottish Society for the Mentally Handicapped.

Measor, J. (1989) 'Are you coming to the dirty films today?', in Holly, L. (Ed) *Girls and Sexuality.* Milton Keynes: Open University.

Monat-Haller, R. (1992) *Understanding and Expressing Sexuality:*

Responsible choices for individuals with developmental disabilities. Baltimore: Paul Brookes Publishing Company.

Owens, G. (1987) 'Radical Behaviourism and the Ethics of Clinical Psychology', in Fairbairn, S. and Fairbairn, G. (Eds) *Psychology, Ethics and Change.* London: Routledge and Kegan Paul.

Perske, R. and Perske, M. (1988) *Circles of Friends.* Nashville: Abingdon Press.

Potter, D. (1976) *Brimstone and Treacle.* (Screened August 1987).

Righton, P. (1981) 'The Adult', in Taylor, B. *Perspectives on Paedophilia.* London, Batsford Academic.

Sgroi, S. (1989) *Vulnerable Populations: Sexual Abuse Treatment for Children, Adult Survivors, Offenders, and Persons with Mental Retardation.* Lexington: Lexington Books.

Turk, V. and Brown, H. (1992) 'Sexual Abuse and Adults with Learning Diffficulties', *Mental Handicap*, 20,2 (June1992), 56–58.

Wald, M. (1982) 'State intervention on behalf of endangered children: a proposed legal response', *International Journal of Child Abuse and Neglect*, 16, 3–45.

Wittgenstein, L. (1974) *Philosophical Investigations.* tr. Anscombe, G.E.M., Oxford: Basil Blackwell.

Wolfensberger, W. (1972) *The Principle of Normalisation in Human Services.* Toronto: National Institute for Mental Retardation.

Wolfensberger, W. (1983) 'Social Role Valorisation: A Proposed New Term for the Principle of Normalisation', *Mental Retardation*, 21, 234–239.

Index

List of occurrence of real and imagined characters in the stories
In discussing the stories through which we have chosen to raise and illustrate the points we make, we refer to many people both real and imagined. In order to facilitate readers in finding their way round the book and the tales we tell, we list these people and where you can read about them below: